iNTRAPRENEURSHIP

IGNITE INNOVATION

Become a Successful Intrapreneur
Recruit and Retain Key Employees
Unlock New Product Creation
Expand Market Share
Sustain Higher Profits
Improve Job Satisfaction

"Whatever the mind can conceive and believe it can achieve."
~Napoleon Hill

Howard Edward Haller, Ph.D.

Published by Silver Eagle Press, Coeur d'Alene, Idaho

ISBN: 1-60655-001-2
ISBN-13: 978-1-60655-001-4

DEDICATION

To the luminary leaders and best-selling authors who peer debriefed my leadership doctoral dissertation and who's insightful quotes throughout the chapters of this book. Thank you again to:
Dr. Ken Blanchard, Jack Canfield, Dr. John Kotter,
Professor James M Kouzes, and Dr. Meg Wheatley

Special thanks to my mentor and graduate school professor,
Dr. Peter Drucker, who inspired me with these thoughts:

"If you want something new, you have to stop doing something old."

"This defines entrepreneur and entrepreneurship ~the entrepreneur always searches for change, responds to it, and exploits it as an opportunity."

"Business has only two functions — marketing and innovation."

And a personal "Thank you" to the executives and Board of Directors of PR1ME Computer Inc., Anaconda-Ericsson Inc., and Corona Data Systems. These visionaries embraced intrapreneurship and authorized, empowered, and encouraged me to successfully create intrapreneurial divisions or subsidiaries within their corporations which collectively resulted in nearly $1 Billion in sales.

CONTENTS

About the Author

IGNITE INNOVATION TODAY!

Corporate executives who lead and build powerful teams and organizational cultures that support game-changing innovation agree. Out-of-the-box thinking, risk taking, and the drive of entrepreneurship need to resonate loud and clear within their organizations.

Dr. Haller goes beyond concept and theory of intrapreneurship. As a proven "hands on" intrapreneurship expert, he has taken multiple intrapreneurial ventures, as founder or co-founder, from Zero in sales to over Hundreds of Millions of dollars in sales-each in four years or less. Haller successfully built a series of profitable intrapreneurial (corporate entrepreneurial) entities within large, medium, and small companies. Some of these include: PR1ME Computer, Anaconda-Ericsson Inc., and Corona Data Systems.

Called "The da Vinci of Finance" by those who know him, Dr. Haller is on a mission to light the spark and to nourish the flame of intrapreneurship by creating a million intrapreneurs, who are beating the drum for a way to create innovation within the confines of cubicle nation in a way it's never been done before, to make the world a better place.

Visit: **IntrapreneurshipSpeaker.com** today!

Chapter 1

INTRAPRENEURSHIP VS ENTREPRENEURSHIP

"Cherish your visions and your dreams, as they are the children of your soul; the blueprints of your ultimate achievements."
~Napoleon Hill

Entrepreneurs/Intrapreneurs: Unlocking Innovation

These days, most of us are familiar with entrepreneurs even if we are not exactly sure what the term means. Jeff Bezos walked away from a successful job with a hedge fund in 1992 to start up a radical new kind of retailing operation called Amazon.com. Fred Smith turned a Yale University C- term paper into FedEx, and Howard Schultz parlayed a love of coffee into Starbucks. As other successful entrepreneurs of this and earlier ages, they each created something of great value by bringing together a unique combination of resources to exploit a market opportunity, usually at great risk to their careers and their finances.

Entrepreneurs and intrapreneurs are both innovators and integral to the process of invention. They generate exciting new ideas and solutions that benefit their corporations. They are consistently creating ideas for products and services that are unique, new, relevant, and important for its existence. These products and services fulfill the needs of their clients within a specific market or society. Innovation propels companies forward, boosts their profitability, and allows them to expand and grow at a faster rate.

The entrepreneur is an individual *who organizes and operates a business through taking personal and financial risk.* Entrepreneurs are innovators themselves. Many times they assume the role of CEO within their own corporations and encourage intrapreneurship to generate new cash flow opportunities and to grow their companies. They may strengthen their profitability through the acquisition of smaller companies, integrating their assets into their own, or through the establishment of a new division or a startup within their corporations.

The intrapreneur is an individual *within an organization or company* who creates and/or takes responsibility for transforming an idea into a profitable venture through taking an innovative approach. Intrapreneurs sometimes work for corporations that are owned by entrepreneurs. Some of these entrepreneurs encourage and allow innovation to occur through intrapreneurship and monetarily support the establishment of new ventures that will bring future profitability to the corporation. Sir Richard Branson, Ken Kutaragi, and Steve Jobs are examples of entrepreneurs/intrapreneurs who understood the importance of intrapreneurship to create and sustain successful corporations that compete and thrive in the global economy.

Intrapreneurial Ventures: The Difference

"The great leaders are like the best conductors; they reach beyond the notes to reach the magic in the player." ~Blaine Lee

Why are some products, services, or divisions of business considered intrapreneurial ventures while others are not? The difference is where the idea for the new product, or service or division originates. *In most corporate settings, new ideas originate in the "ivory tower" of organizational bureaucracy,* in other words, **from the top down**. Only those few folks in the C-suite will have access to the company's business decisions.

Even those in supervisory roles can be blindsided by unexpected announcements, new initiatives, and policy changes. Management explains what needs to be created and employees comply without question. Employees have no voice about what, how, or why any new products or services are created within a company. If a new division is to be created, company management will create the division and will either hire from outside the organization or promote from within, but in all cases any forward movement of new products, services, or divisions are a corporate decision.

Existing rules and policies in bureaucratic companies can put a damper on new ideas. Forbes Contributor, Steve Denning makes this observation, "Bureaucracy is aimed at producing average products and services efficiently. It's not agile enough to delight anyone-either the people doing the work or the people for whom the work is being done. So it's not that bureaucracy is inherently bad. It's just that bureaucracy doesn't fit today's world."

The idea for an intrapreneurial venture comes **from the bottom up**. In other words, the idea for new products, services, or divisions, may originate from anywhere within the corporate structure. Any employee from any division within these enlightened companies is allowed to suggest ideas for new products, services, divisions, or markets. If the employee's idea is accepted, these companies have systems in place to help bring the new idea to fruition. The company will back the creative intrapreneurial team with company resources such as time, money, and technical help. Teams tend to be smaller and will only report to a few to executives, allowing them to become more agile. Global competition and the availability of instant information have resulted in a fundamental shift in power from seller to buyer. Intrapreneurial ventures allow a company to become more fluid and react faster to buyer's wishes and demands. Companies that are managed with the principles of intrapreneurship such as Apple, Virgin, Amazon, Google, and Intuit recognize massive financial gains.

Skunk Works® Intrapreneurial Venture

"In this volatile business of ours, we can ill afford to rest on our laurels, even to pause in retrospect. Times and conditions change so rapidly that we must keep our aim constantly focused on the future." ~Walt Disney

While the term intrapreneurship may be relatively new, the corporate entrepreneurship concept has been in practice in progressive companies as far back as the 1940's. During World War II the U.S. Army's Air Tactical Service Command (ATSC) met with the Lockheed Aircraft Corporation to express its dire need for a jet fighter. Clarence "Kelly" L. Johnson (a Lockheed engineer) assembled a hand-picked team of Lockheed Aircraft Corporation engineers and manufacturing people to rapidly create the XP~80 Fighter project for the U.S. Army. Only one month later his team of bright young engineers hand delivered their XP~80 Shooting Star Jet Fighter proposal to the ATSC who immediately gave the green light for Lockheed to start.

There was no space available at the Lockheed facility for Johnson's "Skunk Works®" group. However, this lack of space at "Corporate" actually worked in the "Skunk Works®" favor and gave them autonomy from traditional "by the book" Lockheed engineers. This ability to eliminate corporate "red tape" allowed Johnson and his "Skunk Works®" team to create and operate effectively and efficiently. They designed and built the XP~80 in only 143 days (Seven days before the due day to ATSC.)

Intrapreneurship in Practice

"Your work is going to fill a large part of your life, and the only way to be truly satisfied is to do what you believe is great work. And the only way to do great work is to love what you do. If you haven't found it yet, keep looking. Don't settle. As with all matters of the heart, you'll know when you find it." ~Steve Jobs

Successful companies encourage their employees to think out-of-the-box in order to fuel the growth of their businesses. Free flowing ideas frequently generated from their employees may become the next big product to be sold in a new and emerging market. New innovations, whether it is a new product or service, gives a corporation a competitive advantage within their industry.

From the very beginning Apple adopted vertical integration as part of its business process, making Apple and its products different from other manufacturers in the market. That was a main reason Macintosh came with an integrated OS, designed and developed by Apple itself. Mac OS is now considered as one of the leading OS's in the computing industry. Macintosh was manufactured as a PC (Personal Computer) that was designed mostly for creative professionals, home users, and students. Even after the ups and downs of Apple's business Mac is still the first choice of many professionals and personal computer users.

3M is a beacon of intrapreneurship and is considered to be one of the most innovative companies in the not only the U. S. but the entire world. Through its intrapreneurial "Bootlegging Policy," (which allows employees to spend up to 15 percent of their time at work developing their own creative ideas for the betterment of the company and the creation of new products or services) 3M allows an employee-intrapreneur limited freedom to pursue new ideas.

Other business leaders are beginning to recognize the benefits that can be derived by encouraging employees to turn their own ideas into profitable products or services. The process, known as intrapreneurship, has since been responsible for the development of a wide array of successful new cutting-edge offerings from companies as diverse as Google, Anaconda-Ericsson Inc., DreamWorks, PR1ME Computer, Inc., GE, Hilton, Yahoo!, Sony, W. L. Gore, Intel, LinkedIn, and more.

Change Makers: Forever Changing the Face of Innovation

"You see things; and you say 'Why?' But I dream things that never were; and I say 'Why not?" ~*George Bernard Shaw*

Entrepreneurs and intrapreneurs are constantly making profound change both outside and within their organizations through the process of innovation. Sir Richard Branson, Ken Kutaragi, and Steve Jobs each demonstrated their ingenuity and creativity to the world through the establishment of new companies and effectively used intrapreneurship for the continual invention and improvement of products and services.

They also developed strong skills in team building and management through their varied corporate experiences. These two skills are important to possess in order for innovation within a corporation to be successful. Employees need strong role models who will teach them and support them along the way. They need to be able to look up to innovators who already possess the expertise and who will inspire and motivate them to flourish under their guidance.

ENTREPRENEURS AND INTRAPRENEURS ARE BOTH INNOVATORS AND INTEGRAL TO THE PROCESS OF INVENTION. THEY GENERATE EXCITING NEW IDEAS, PRODUCTS, AND SOLUTIONS.

THE QUESTION IS: DO YOU WANT THESE VISIONARIES WORKING FOR YOU, OR AS THE COMPETITION?

Chapter 2

12 STRATEGIES FOR INTRAPRENEURIAL SUCCESS

"You have to learn the rules of the game. Then you have to play better than anyone else." ~Albert Einstein

As an intrapreneur, it is essential that you be able to recognize opportunity, evaluate pros and cons, and justify your reasoning to your management team. You must learn to be bold and present well thought out ideas with confidence and conviction. You'll pursue new and different opportunities that help to guide your company into unfamiliar territory and open the doors to new revenue streams in the process.

If you are an intrapreneur you are a natural problem solver who helps your company create solutions to existing problems when needed. You are the voice of reason as well as the voice of innovation. Through you expertise you can guide your organization in making informative decisions. Intrapreneurship allows employees like you to be part of the decision making process. Your company will benefit by allowing intrapreneurs like you to share different points of view. The company may not see that a problem has multiple solutions. But through sharing and collaboration collective decisions can be made. If you wish to be a successful intrapreneur, there are 12 strategies you can use to help ensure success.

Accept Risks
"The most valuable thing you can make is a mistake ~you can't learn anything from being perfect." ~Adam Osborne

Intrapreneurs take initiative and come up with new ideas and new methods for doing things. Run it by management with confidence and be open to the opportunity of learning why the manager might be opposed to the idea. There may be other ideas floating around in the corporation of which you may not be aware. If more research is needed, take it as a new challenge, a new opportunity for growth and greater job security.

Find Solutions For Unknown Or Unsolved Problems
"I try to learn from the past, but I plan for the future by focusing exclusively on the present. That's where the fun is."
~Donald Trump

Staying a step ahead of the game is vital to being successful in your intrapreneurial endeavors. If you find several solutions, weigh the pros and cons of each with management. Problem solving is a requirement in becoming a successful intrapreneur.

Maintain A Positive Attitude
"Every strike brings me closer to the next home run." ~Babe Ruth

Intrapreneurs thrive when they have a positive attitude. No one enjoys working with someone who is skeptical or negative. This creates a bad apple in the barrel of employees. Having a positive attitude is contagious and creates stronger bonds with those you work with and those you work for.

Motivate, Motivate, Motivate
"Good business leaders create a vision, articulate the vision, passionately own the vision, and relentlessly drive it to completion." ~Jack Welch

Encourage everyone around you so they begin to realize you are a strong support system. This creates trust and dependability, not to mention a much smoother work flow. Help those on your intrapreneurial team. They have quotas and goals to achieve and are more dependent on you than you may think. Help them get to where they need to be to become successful. They will always see your inspiration and motivation.

Gain Knowledge

"I like to think of innovation as upgrading your current self. This upgrade helps you to more effectively deal with changes happening around you and to be able to think in a more complex manner than before." ~Daniel Willey

To be recognized as an intrapreneurial leader, it is important to do the research required to provide viable guidance and suggestions to guide the course of new products, services, or process creation. Ask questions and do what is needed in order for you to fully understand the vision and mission statement of the organization. Don't help it only achieve the vision, help to surpass it. Go beyond what is expected of you. Giving your all to an organization is what makes great leaders and great intrapreneurs. Use all your talents and skills to help grow the organization.

Take Initiative and Innovate

"Do not follow where the path may lead. Go instead where there is no path and leave a trail." ~Ralph Waldo Emerson

To move up the ladder within your organization you need to demonstrate the positive attributes and business sense required for the level you are working to achieve. Lead discussions via email and in meetings. To prompt a group to think of a situation with a new perspective, ask open-ended questions. Start with something like, "What would happen if we tried this?"

Create A Relaxed Environment

"To teach that a comparatively few men are responsible for the greatest forward steps of mankind is the worst sort of nonsense." ~Henry Ford

Intrapreneurs set the stage for creativity and teamwork. Innovation and brilliance can often be found in the least suspected places, from the janitorial and maintenance staff upwards. Many of these people know the job inside and out and can often suggest solutions that may surprise you. Be open, positive, encouraging, trustworthy, and supportive.

Set The Stage For A Synergistic Environment

"If one advances confidently in the direction of his dreams, and endeavors to live the life which he has imagined, he will meet with a success unexpected in common hours."
~Henry David Thoreau

Be empathetic. People can be resistant to change. The reason can be as simple as not perceiving the desired result or the role they will play in a new endeavor. Ask for their ideas. Help them to understand how important their ideas and concerns are. Everyone will begin to see that the greater whole is not complete or as powerful as the total sum of its parts. Stay focused on objectives. Take leadership in the innovation and execution phases.

Communicate Regularly

"The best way to get a good idea is to have a lot of ideas."
~Linus Pauling

Intrapreneur leadership requires trust, dependability, and maintaining an open relationship. Keep communication lines open to those above you and with those with whom you work.

Analyze Outcomes and Make Adjustments

"Man, alone, has the power to transform his thoughts into physical reality; man, alone, can dream and make his dreams come true." *~Napoleon Hill*

Realize that being innovative means taking risks. If something fails, look carefully at every aspect of it to see what you can learn from it. Opportunities are everywhere you look. Do not limit your thinking.

Plant A Seed Of Suggestion

"A mediocre idea that generates enthusiasm will go further than a great idea that inspires no one." *~Mary Kay Ash*

See if it begins to become nourished for growth and implementation. Seeds you sow in this position foster a learning environment for everyone. As an intrapreneur, do more than just plant a seed of suggestions. Champion innovative ideas for new products, services, or processes.

Implement Solutions

"Without leaps of imagination, or dreaming, we lose the excitement of possibilities. Dreaming, after all, is a form of planning." ~Gloria Steinem

Intrapreneurs will find there are many paths to achieve the same result. Look over each one carefully with an open-mind. Find the best path that will benefit the organization, your manager, and yourself. Remember, intrapreneurs are the champions or their innovative creations within their organizations and the company as a whole.

IF YOU ARE AN INTRAPRENEUR YOU CAN GUIDE YOUR ORGANIZATION IN MAKING INFORMATIVE DECISIONS. INTRAPRENEURSHIP ALLOWS YOU TO BE PART OF THE DECISION MAKING PROCESS.

INTRAPRENEURSHIP

Chapter 3

9 HABITS OF HIGHLY EFFECTIVE AND SUCCESSFUL INTRAPRENEURS

"The very essence of leadership is that you have a vision. It's got to be a vision you articulate clearly and forcefully on every occasion. You can't blow an uncertain trumpet."
~Theodore Hesburgh

Intrapreneurs generate inventive ideas that create escalating and enduring success for an organization.

Are you an intrapreneur? Do you demonstrate these traits?

Are You a Trail Blazer or Maverick?

"Implementing best practice is copying yesterday, innovation is inventing tomorrow." ~Paul Sloane

Realize that being innovative means taking calculated risks. For intrapreneurs to be a true trail blazer or maverick sometimes means ignoring the rules or breaking the rules to get things done. You will come up with new ideas, new methods for doing things. Look at the upside and downside of any decision.

Are You an Out-Of-The-Box Thinker?

"It isn't all over; everything has not been invented; the human adventure is just beginning." ~*Gene Roddenberry*

Opportunities are everywhere in every organization. Do you see things from a different perspective and are you willing to create solutions and uncover problems within the organization. Stay a step ahead of the game to be successful. Embrace surprises because they provide greater opportunity for innovation. Don't only think out-of-the-box, but get rid of the box!

Can You Create Unique and Useful Products or Services?

"For the most part, the best opportunities now lie where your competitors have yet to establish themselves, not where they're already entrenched. Microsoft is struggling to adapt to that new reality." ~*Paul Allen*

As an intrapreneur, you will generate new ideas and then promote them internally and guide them to a successful conclusion. When we talk about innovation we're generally referring to a shiny new object or a powerful new process or service. There are many paths that will achieve the same result. Always be learning and trying new ideas that can create new products or services, enter new markets, and innovate. Consider each new idea carefully with an open-mind. Think: How can this help my company grow?

Do You Solve Important Problems and Find Solutions?

"Creativity dies in an indisciplined environment."
~*James C. Collins*

Intrapreneurs approach decision making differently. Challenge yourself and your team to come up with new products and services and look beyond your own defined circle of responsibility for ways to make them happen. Find the best path for the solution to be implemented that will benefit the organization. Find, recruit, and encourage team members who will take time to explore and provide more solutions to complex problems. Problem solving is a requirement in becoming a great intrapreneur.

Are You Self-Motivated?

"An extraordinary person is someone who consistently does the things ordinary people can't do or won't do." ~Nido R. Qubein

Intrapreneurs take action and follow through with their ideas. You may not be the one that comes up with an idea but you are one who can take an idea and turn it into a viable business. You will take your organization's goals and strategies and make them your goals and strategies. You'll take time to find out what matters to the decision makers in your company and create accordingly. Intrapreneurs are decisive.

Are You Persistent?

"Most great people have attained their greatest success just one step beyond their greatest failure." ~Napoleon Hill

Do not wait for everything to be perfect before making a decision. Deal with uncertainty by acting on it, not sitting back and waiting to see what happens. Elbert Hubbard said, "A little more persistence, a little more effort, and what seemed a hopeless failure may turn to glorious success." Understand that all reasonable intrapreneurial efforts have to keep moving along without negatively impacting regular company duties. Don't let things drag. Set milestones to keep yourself and your team on track.

Are You a Team Player?

"I am in no sense of the word a great artist, not even a great animator; I have always had men working for me whose skills were greater than my own. I am an idea man." —Walt Disney

Intrapreneurs create a relaxed environment to set the stage to encourage innovation, creativity and teamwork. Co-workers may often suggest surprising solutions which need to be acknowledged. Prompt groups to think of a situation with a new perspective; ask open-ended questions. Allow time for inner reflection on how to "solve" a problem or how to create a new product or service. Give yourself and your team time to regularly have brainstorm or "hackathon" sessions. Innovation, creativity, and brilliance can be found in the least suspected places. Encourage open sharing of new ideas. Publicize and share ongoing efforts. Co-workers who hears about the new idea may provide the "missing link" that brings it to fruition. As an intrapreneur, take charge of leading discussions via email and in meetings. True intrapreneurs are trustworthy, encouraging, open, creative, innovative, positive, supportive, and give credit where it's due!

Are You Discouraged by Setbacks or Failure?

"Remember the two benefits of failure. First, if you do fail, you learn what doesn't work; and second, the failure gives you the opportunity to try a new approach." ~Roger Von Oech

In spite of setbacks, intrapreneurs maintain a positive attitude. An intrapreneurial effort can be challenging even though it is officially encouraged and no personal capital is at risk. If something fails, look carefully at every aspect of it to see what you can learn from it. Thomas A. Edison said, "I have not failed 10,000 times. I have successfully found 10,000 ways that will not work." A positive attitude is contagious and creates stronger bonds with those who work for you and for those with whom you work.

Do You Think Like An Entrepreneur, Not An Employee?

"The best vision is insight." ~Malcolm Forbes

Do research, ask questions, and do what is needed to fully understand the vision and mission statement of the organization. Create a unique niche or sub organization. Help not only achieve the vision of your company but help to surpass it. Go beyond what is expected of you. True intrapreneurs will give their all to an organization to become innovators and leaders. Your talents and skills can help grow your organization.

OPPORTUNITIES ARE EVERYWHERE. LOOK FOR THOSE INDIVIDUALS WHO SEE THINGS FROM A DIFFERENT PERSPECTIVE AND WHO WILL CREATE SOLUTIONS AND UNCOVER PROBLEMS WITHIN THE ORGANIZATION.

iΠTRᴀPRENEURSHIP

Chapter 4

3 FAMOUS INTRAPRENEURS

"A leader's role is to raise people's aspirations for what they can become and to release their energies so they will try to get there."
~David Gergen

Sir Richard Branson and the Virgin Group

"Few entrepreneurs -- scratch that: almost no one -- ever achieved anything worthwhile without help. To be successful in business, you need to connect and collaborate and delegate."
~Sir Richard Branson

Sir Richard Branson, founder and CEO of Virgin Group, LTD, is an entrepreneur who values innovation, intrapreneurship, and entrepreneurship within his own corporation. His corporation, the Virgin Group, LTD., is a British investment group or multinational branded venture capital group. Its core ventures include entertainment, travel, and lifestyle. The Virgin Group consists of over 400 companies around the globe. Sir Richard Branson encourages his team to use intrapreneurship to help grow the Virgin Group. The healthy growth of a corporation, in his eyes, needs intrapreneurs.

Sir Richard Branson started his first record shop in London, England in 1971 and dubbed it "Virgin Records." The name "Virgin" came to mind because he and one of his employees realized that they were virgins in the record business. The Virgin music label was established with his partner Nik Powell in 1972 after the company had made enough money from the record store. It was at this time that he bought a country estate and converted it into a recording studio where he leased out recording time to new artists and music groups. They also signed a number of artists and music groups to their label.

The Virgin brand grew rapidly in the 1980s while expanding Virgin records and establishing Virgin Atlantic Airways in 1984. Branson established Virgin Mobile in 1999, Virgin Blue (Australia) in 2000, and Virgin Trains in 1993. He acquired a few struggling airline companies and established Virgin Express, Virgin America, and Virgin Nigeria. Virgin Galactic was established by the Virgin group in 2004 to provide private citizens the opportunity for sub-orbital travel to the edge of the Earth's atmosphere and space for $200,000 a ticket. In 2013, Delta Airlines purchased 49% of Singapore Airlines for $360million from Virgin Atlantic. Virgin Atlantic founder, Sir Richard Branson, will retain his 51% stake.

Sir Richard is an entrepreneur and self-made multi-billionaire who actively supports intrapreneurship. These beliefs have helped him build an estimated worth of over $4.6 billion. He retains control of the Virgin brand, and each of the companies within the company are separate entities.

In a published article Sir Richard Branson discussed his views on the importance of intrapreneurs and intrapreneurship. He mentions that corporate executives and entrepreneurs must empower their intrapreneurs to "break the rules." Intrapreneurs are given freedom and monetary support to develop a new product, system, or service and they do not have to follow the corporation's usual routines. He also sees entrepreneurs as the catalysts that get corporations started, while intrapreneurs drive the corporations into new and unexpected areas of business.

Steve Jobs, Apple, Inc. and Innovation in Technology

"For the past 33 years, I have looked in the mirror every morning and asked myself: 'If today were the last day of my life, would I want to do what I am about to do today?' And whenever the answer has been 'No' for too many days in a row, I know I need to change something" ~Steve Jobs

Steve Jobs, called himself a "hopeless romantic" who wanted to make a profound difference in the world. His vision was to create, in his words, "a computer for the rest of us." A computer that anyone could afford and he fit the roles of both intrapreneur and entrepreneur perfectly. He had a deep understanding about how a corporation could excel using the talent they already possess. He created a successful corporate empire with Co-Founder Steve Wozniak that revolutionized the technology industry forever.

Steve Jobs successfully used intrapreneurship and leaves an amazing legacy behind, both as an entrepreneur and an intrapreneur.

Steve Jobs is the ultimate intrapreneur. Jobs, together with Apple, has made revolutionary technologies available to the world. His innovation and creativity has helped propel Apple into the foreground as a leader in the computer industry. His quest began along with Steve Wozniak in the development of Apple's first computer in 1976. Jobs worked at Atari as a game designer and Wozniak worked for Hewlett Packard when they created the first personal computer. Under the terms of his employment contract, Wozniak had to present Hewlett Packard with the prototype of his personal computer. It was rejected by an HP executive at the time. The executive wondered, "What, if anything, a regular person would do with a computer." Wozniak happily resigned from the corporation so he could partner with Jobs to focus entirely on establishing Apple, Inc. Their collective vision was to get a computer into the hands of everyday people, and they succeeded beyond their wildest dreams.

Steve Jobs and Apple Co-Founder Steve Wozniak started Apple, Inc., in 1976, from the comfort and convenience of Jobs' family home. The first 50 Apple computers were built in the garage. His sister Patty fondly recollects being one of Jobs' many helpers and assembling circuit boards in their living room. This was the place where Jobs and his father would spend countless nights taking apart and reconstructing electronics when he was a child. He also worked on his first high school project involving the assembly of a computer using Hewlett Packard parts in this garage. Today, the family home in Mountain View, Silicon Valley, California is currently being reviewed by the city of Palo Alto as a historic site.

In the 1980s, Steve Jobs selected 20 talented Apple engineers to assist him with the development of the Apple Macintosh computer or the "Mac" computer. Under his supervision, this "MAC" group independently designed and created the computers without any interference from then CEO John Sculley and the Apple Board of Directors. The Macintosh computer was released in 1984. It was the first computer with an interface that was graphical and that was controlled with a mouse. The MAC computer was an innovation breakthrough in the world of computers and competed directly with computers produced by their new rival the IBM PC.

Unfortunately, the Macintosh computer failed to meet financial projections due to the way it was marketed. The Mac that Steve Jobs envisioned was priced out of the range for a home computer. In addition it did not contain any features that corporations could use in their day to day business operations. Lack of networking features, memory, and no hard drive made the Macintosh a failure to the board of directors. It caused a decline in sales and profits and almost half of their market was lost to IBM during this period. Although the Macintosh was a marketing nightmare, it was the forerunner for all the successive Apple computers that would be created in the future. It was the first computer on the market that offered a user friendly interface that became the standard for the computer industry.

The decline in profits from the Macintosh combined with disappointing sales of the Apple III and the LISA caused major friction between Steve Jobs, and the Board of Directors at Apple. Members of the Apple Board of Directors, John Scully, CEO and especially Arthur Rock, a venture capitalist, became increasingly irritated with Jobs' style of leadership. They witnessed that the products created by the Mac group were in direct competition with Apple's products. They became increasingly unhappy with the independent nature of the intrapreneurship and lack of direct control over what Steve Jobs was doing at the time. Unwilling to support the venture and the intrapreneurship efforts demonstrated by Jobs as a leader, the Board removed him from his seat on the board. More ironic was the fact that Jobs had personally selected John Sculley, from PepsiCo to assist him in running the operations at Apple. Sculley, Rock, and the Apple Board of Directors took away Jobs' authority, rendering him powerless. Jobs resigned from Apple and then sold his stock in the corporation.

Steve Jobs and His Legacy

Steve Jobs helped to popularize the term "intrapreneur" in the mid~1980s. According to the article written in the September 30, 1985 of Newsweek, Jobs stated that, "The Macintosh team was what is commonly known as intrapreneurship; a group of people going, in essence, back to the garage, but in a large company." This infamous statement referred to the fact that Apple, Inc., an industry leader, was started in the childhood home of co-founder Steve Jobs.

Several weeks later, Steve later returned to the corporation as a consultant and later become the Chairman of Apple. He revived the financially struggling corporation and propelled it into the future. He saved the company he founded with the design and creation of the iPod, iTunes, iPad, iPhone, and the iCloud through the use of intrapreneurship. He again selected a group of talented employees like he had done in the past, and through his mentoring, leadership and dedication, he and his team overcame tough times and ensured the future of Apple. Many consumers of Apple products such as the iPhone still line up outside Mac stores throughout the country and camp out all night because they desire to be the first to purchase the newest version of their products when they are released. Some products may not be available for weeks or months or sometimes need to be pre-ordered a month in advance. The impact Apple has had worldwide is incredible.

The legacy of Steve Jobs lives on within the corporate fabric of intrapreneurship. He has been immortalized as a genius, an inventor, an entrepreneur, as well as an intrapreneur. His passion for innovation and determination for Apple products to be the gold standard in the industry will forever be revered and emulated for years to come. He was at the forefront of cutting edge technology and made it available and affordable to the masses worldwide. His legacy lives on in every product Apple has made and will make. His legacy also lives on in every client's use and enjoyment of Apple products.

Ken Kutaragi, and the Creation of the Sony PlayStation

"Failure defeats losers, failure inspires winners."
~Robert T. Kiyosaki

An educated electrical engineer, Ken joined Sony Corporation in Japan in 1975 at the age of 25. Ken was working in the sound labs at Sony Corporation when he bought his young daughter a Nintendo game console. Ken observed his daughter playing with a Famicom, the new Nintendo game but he was displeased with the quality of the sound of the Nintendo game. Because of his training and experience in electronics Ken concluded that a digital chip, dedicated solely to sound, would significantly improve the quality of the Nintendo gaming system.

Because the Sony Corporation was not currently involved in computer games Ken negotiated to keep his job at Sony while working as an outside consultant (entrepreneur) for Nintendo on their computer gaming devices. Ken developed the "SPC7000" for the next generation of Nintendo games and machines. Senior executives at Sony Corporation threatened to fire him after they discovered his sideline project with Nintendo, even though it had previously been approved by Sony's middle managers.

Fortunately for Ken he had strong support of Norio Ohga (CEO of Sony Corporation at the time). Chairman Ohga personally recognized the value of Ken's creativity, entrepreneurial spirit, and innovation, so he encouraged Kutaragi's efforts. With the Sony Corporation CEO's support (and begrudgingly the rest of Sony's senior and middle management's blessing) Kutaragi continued to work as a part-time consultant to Nintendo. Ken successfully developed a CD-ROM-based system for Nintendo.

Then in a life changing twist of fate Nintendo elected not to go forward with the CD-ROM system. Ken Kutaragi saw the market and business opportunity of computer gaming systems for Sony. With his intrapreneurial spirit Ken pressed hard to convince the Sony Corporation to enter the electronic gaming business.

While most of Sony's senior management did not consider Ken's computer gaming device more than a toy and not worthwhile for Sony. Chairman Ohga took a major chance and backed Kutaragi's plan. Ken was persistent and led the effort to help Sony develop its own gaming system, the blockbuster product success "PlayStation." Ken Kutaragi has been often been referred to as "The Father of the PlayStation" as well as all related Sony products including Sony PlayStation 2, Sony PlayStation Portable, Sony PlayStation 3, and the current Sony PlayStation 4.

Ken Kutaragi fought against all the corporate "naysayers" within Sony's management ranks. As an intrapreneur, Ken literally laid his job on the line at Sony to press for the creation of the computer gaming product within Sony. Ken is credited with saying, "I wanted to prove that even [when] regular company employees said no, [and] especially regular company employees -[I] could build a venture of this scale with superb technology, superb concepts, and superb colleagues."

Sony's "System G" 3~D technology, aka Sony PlayStation, was released in 1994. It immediately outsold Nintendo's Super NES to quickly become the world's top home-gaming platform. Ken's group within Sony did not rest on its laurels. Kutaragi and Sony took another major financial gamble on PlayStation 2. Sony backed Ken's intrapreneurial venture by investing $2.5 billion into the PlayStation start-up which soon owned over 70% of the home-video-game-console international market share.

Sony's PlayStation product line had become the leading video-game platform. The financial payback to Sony was astronomical. At of the end 1997, the first four years of the PlayStation product line existence, Sony's PlayStation annual sales grew to $7 Billion. Ken's intrapreneurial success has been called one of the greatest new business creations and launches in business history. The new Sony's intrapreneurially created product line outperformed both the Nintendo and Sega Enterprises gaming machines.

The Sony PlayStation took the clear market share of game consoles with PlayStation sales of more than 70 million units in the late 1990's. At that time one in four United States households owned a Sony PlayStation product. The strong profits from the Sony PlayStation line accounted for about one quarter of the overall Sony Corporation's profits.

Sony Computer Entertainment, Inc. shared that PlayStation 4 has cumulatively sold through more than 7 million units globally as of April 6th, 2014. PS4 software sales are another bright spot, with more than 20.5 million copies sold at retail and PlayStation Store worldwide as of April 13th, 2014. But, that was just the beginning of the PlayStation 4 success story in 2014.

During his Keynote at the January 2015 Consumer Electronics Show Sony CEO Kazuo Hirai announced that the company's PlayStation 4sold more than 4.1 million units during this holiday season and total sales so far have been 18.5 million units. PlayStation Online now boasts 10.9 million subscribers.

"The success of PlayStation 4 has enabled a new world for PlayStation," Hirai said. "Together with third-party developers, the company will continue to provide Sony's signature 'wow' to valued customers. The entertainment company debuted the PlayStation 4 in 2013 as a competitor to Microsoft's XBox One."

Ken has left a last and enduring legacy as a successful Intrapreneur.

Kutaragi was rewarded for his significant success as an intrapreneur within Sony. Ken was promoted to be the Chairman and CEO of Sony Computer Entertainment (SCEI), the video game division of Sony. As Chairman and CEO, Kutaragi built Sony Computer Entertainment group into a major profit center for the Sony Corporation. This is an amazing result of the successful use of intrapreneurship. At the Game Developer's Choice Awards, Ken was awarded the Lifetime Achievement Award.

"It's not what the vision is; it's what the vision does."
~Peter Senge

Chapter 5

BENEFITS TO INTRAPRENEURIAL EMPLOYEES: INCREASED JOB SATISFACTION

"You have to decide what your highest priorities are and have the courage—pleasantly, smilingly, non-apologetically, to say "no" to other things. And the way you do that is by having a bigger "yes" burning inside. The enemy of the "best" is often the "good."
~Stephen R. Covey

Intrapreneurship Creates a Win-Win Situation for both intrapreneurs and the enlightened companies for which they work.

Intrapreneurial ventures would not work if employees involved did not see and realize tremendous personal and professional value from it. Fortunately, they do. Such intrapreneurial ventures allow people in any organization to tap into personnel and other various resources in order to be creative and think out-of-the-box on company time. By helping satisfy the "inherent self-actualization needs" identified by noted psychologist Abraham Maslow, intrapreneurship creates a win-win situation for employer and employee alike.

The most important resource a corporation possesses is its employees and its human capital and the combined intellect they possess. Key individuals make it possible for corporations to operate on a day to day basis, are responsible for innovation, make important decisions, and solve problems. Intrapreneurs are individuals who are willing to take on a certain level of risk to innovate and create and then help build new successful businesses or products from within the corporate structure. Intrapreneurs are the change makers, the trail blazers, the innovators, and the mavericks that drive the direction of their business and facilitate the expansion and growth of their organizations into new and vast frontiers. They are the new leaders of today and tomorrow, keeping their eyes on both the present and the future viability of their companies.

"When the trust account is high, communication is easy, instant, and effective." ~Stephen R. Covey

Intrapreneurs are talented and empowered employees who enable corporations to strategically transform and change the direction of their businesses. Corporations and organization use intrapreneurs to transmit their corporate philosophy and their values within their social business structures. Many global corporations have built and maintained successful and profitable intrapreneurship programs to focus on the satisfaction and retention of their employees. They understand that the viability and profitability of their corporations is directly related to employee satisfaction. They recognize that in order to foster a sense of fulfillment within their employees, it is crucial to build a support system to nurture them.

Intrapreneurship allows organizations to recognize, recruit, and retain key employees. They willingly invest in and develop their human capital. By allowing their employees to grow as intrapreneurs in a supportive environment, they invest their resources in key individuals and their projects. The corporation's confidence in their intrapreneurs motivates them to achieve their goals. Their ventures, in return, are typically more successful and generate profits or a return on the corporation's investment.

This motivates innovators to continually think of, invent, and produce new products and services on a continual basis. This establishes a continuous momentum that once in place is difficult to stop. The momentum of innovation provides a steady stream of income for the corporation that allows them to build their assets and resources. With more assets and resources at their disposal, companies can continuously grow and expand, creating new jobs, and service more clients.

> *"Trust is the glue of life. It's the most essential ingredient in effective communication. It's the foundational principle that holds all relationships." ~Stephen R. Covey*

Intrapreneurship (corporate entrepreneurship) is key to long term success by allowing employees to independently pursue side projects has proven successful for more than 40 years within companies ranging from Lockheed and 3M to Sony and Google. These companies and many like them reap the rewards of new products and new markets along with a more satisfied and productive workforce. Intrapreneurship has been used to create new products and services and increase innovation and profits in the U.S., Canada, South America, Europe, Asia, Africa, and all over the world.

Employers who develop and promote intrapreneurship programs and champion their participants, can expect employees to benefit in a variety of consequential ways. Here are some of the most impactful and effective aspects of intrapreneurship:

- Intrapreneurial employees' creative impulses will be encouraged and maximized. It is said that people who are capable of invention are happiest when they are creating. A company that cultivates a culture of intrapreneurship allows such people to flourish by giving them the space and the tools they need to pursue their dreams without incurring substantial risk. The increased responsibilities and added freedom of movement that result are a big positive for more and more employees these days.

- Intrapreneurship allows key employees to create and operate a startup within an organization instead of independently as an entrepreneur running his or her own company. They are given the necessary resources to be innovative and successful by their company. Intrapreneurs greatly benefit from this symbiotic relationship by not having to assume personal and financial risk while pursuing their innovative business plans and goals. Companies are rewarded with the invention of a new division, product, or startup that boosts the morale and productivity of their employees. Ingenuity, responsibility, and reliability are valued and encouraged characteristics.

- Intrapreneurial employees' successful ventures will be publicly recognized within the company. While employees are not putting their own financial resources or their jobs on the line when they embark on an intrapreneurial venture, they are still in a very real sense risking their reputation and their self-image. As such internal recognition of their efforts, be it praise in a meeting of their peers or a positive report in a companywide publication, will have incalculable positive repercussions. Financial rewards for projects that really hit it out of the park can likewise lift not only the direct beneficiaries but the entire workforce as well.

- Intrapreneurs' growth opportunities will be multiplied. Intrapreneurship can foster collaborative relationships between colleagues, support personnel, managers and other company officials across an entire organization. It increases the visibility of participants and could provide opportunities for internal advancement that might not have arisen otherwise. Those who are motivated to achieve usually see their career paths widen and deepen appreciably.

- Intrapreneurs are typically given more freedom to innovate as well as operate their ventures due to their parent organizations bending of the rules. They are allowed more responsibility, opportunities for decision making, and are reliable individuals who have demonstrated success in the past. They are the employees who pave the way for other employees to follow in their footsteps.

- Employees' job satisfaction will be intensified. There is real pleasure in conceiving, launching, and selling an idea for an innovative product or service that ultimately proves to be a positive for the entire organization. There can even be great opportunities for personal and professional growth realized from initiatives that fail to catch fire. Allowing employees the freedom to create and act on these ideas can make a career much more than "a job."

- Employee intrapreneurs may, and should, be rewarded publicly with plaques or certificates. Inspired organizations may reward an intrapreneur with extra fun time such as an additional vacation for the intrapreneur and their family. Extra performance based pay, bonuses, and promotions are also sound rewards for successful intrapreneurs.

One major benefit to intrapreneurs is that though they do take on a certain amount of risk the amount they take on is significantly less than the average entrepreneur. Intrapreneurs who work within corporations have a financial safety net: supported with financial and material resources from the parent company, they receive a steady paycheck whether the new venture succeeds or fails. They may receive benefits such as health insurance for themselves and their families. Entrepreneurs have to fund their own insurance which affects their bottom line.

Entrepreneurs who start companies on their own risk losing their personal finances, the money and resources they have invested along with any future profits should they go bankrupt or close the doors to their businesses. It is more difficult for an entrepreneur to recover from this type of loss financially and psychologically. Intrapreneurs are somewhat sheltered and protected from this eventuality. If their ventures should fail, their repercussions are not as great as it is for the entrepreneur. Intrapreneurs can pick up where they left off and move on.

"To change ourselves effectively, we first had to change our perceptions." ~Stephen R. Covey

Intrapreneurs will need to keep improving their skills and talents. As these abilities improve, they naturally become the role models for newer innovators within the corporation. They possess the ability to inspire, train, and guide others. Employees who demonstrate innovative thinking and skills are given monetary resources, training, time, and a team of employees to carry their business ventures forward. As a direct result of their involvement in projects such as these, they grow and gain valuable business experience. As proven, reliable and resourceful employees in the past, they are often promoted to leadership positions. In these positions they learn critical skills such as managing employees and resources. In turn, intrapreneurs are able to teach and communicate these skills to their team members and peers .

Organizations, partnerships, non-profits and corporations who have strong intrapreneurship programs can successfully recruit and retain key employees for a longer span of time. Satisfaction is an important factor to the longevity of employees. Intrapreneurial employees who do not have a sense of fulfillment or a certain level of satisfaction, often times, leave a company after a short time for a new experience somewhere else. Some may leave to become the employees of new startups or corporations where their ideas and opinions are appreciated. Some, such as Steve Wozniak, a former employee of Hewlett Packard, become the co-founder of a new corporation, Apple, Inc., and become the competition to HP. This because of the short-sighted executive at Hewlett Packard who rejected the creation of a personal computer.

"Treat a man as he is and he will remain as he is. Treat a man as he can and should be and he will become as he can and should be." ~Stephen R. Covey

Intrapreneurship allows individuals the opportunity to make a profound difference in the corporations for which they presently work. Thirty years after Steve Wozniak left the corporation Hewlett Packard has fully embraced intrapreneurship. They have enacted important company policies to support their intrapreneurs.

The benefits that companies can realize by actively supporting an intrapreneurship effort are many and substantial. The benefits that individual participants can realize are just as significant. In the end, in fact, they may actually provide employers with their program's greatest benefit of all.

MANY GLOBAL CORPORATIONS PARTNERSHIPS, NON-PROFITS, AND LOCAL ORGANIZATIONS UNDERSTAND THAT THE MOST IMPORTANT RESOURCE AN ORGANIZATION POSSESSES IS ITS EMPLOYEES AND THE COMBINED INTELLECT THEY POSSESS.

ORGANIZATIONS THAT HAVE BUILT, SUPPORTED, EMBRACED, AND MAINTAINED PROFITABLE INTRAPRENEURSHIP PROGRAMS TO FOCUS ON THE RECRUITMENT AND RETENTION OF THEIR EMPLOYEES REALIZE THE VIABILITY AND PROFITABILITY OF AN ORGANIZATION IS DIRECTLY RELATED TO EMPLOYEE SATISFACTION.

Chapter 6

ONE TRICKY TRUTH ABOUT INTRAPRENEURSHIP!

"The management methodologies that helped successfully develop enterprises throughout the 20th century are no longer sufficient. Driving results in a world of ever-increasing change requires a new kind of leadership." ~Dr. John Kotter

The Right Leadership is Central for Intrapreneurship!

Given the valuable traits that intrapreneurs possess it is essential that your business is able to identify them and attract them. *The right leadership skills are necessary for your business to motivate its intrapreneurs and to encourage others to follow in their path.*

You can rest assured that potential intrapreneurs are already within your organization or company but they need to be discovered, nurtured, and empowered. Identification of potential intrapreneurs is the first but not the only step to take. Keep in mind that an intrapreneur will display most of the traits that have been discussed so far: strategic scanning and visual thinking, ability to transform creative ideas into innovations, identification with your business goals, a passionate work ethic, etc.

It is the leader's job to learn who those intrapreneurs are and to motivate them in order to unleash their entrepreneurial potential. Once you start identifying and motivating intrapreneurs you will find that more of them will stand out.

The second step intrapreneurial leaders must take is finding the right motivators for intrapreneurs. To do so experts suggest that intrapreneurial employees are given ownership. This means they are given the power to make decisions and to pursue new ideas as well as given clear responsibility and transparency regarding accountability. If you want employees feeling encouraged to experiment and find new business opportunities your company must make risk-taking acceptable and leaders should, in turn, understand that failure is a natural possibility of experimentation and the process that leads up to new ideas.

Intrapreneurs are not careless risk takers, which is why intrapreneurs take ownership and are open to new ideas that are always accompanied by clear goals. The key is to understand that intrapreneurs need a space they feel comfortable in, yet leaders should make sure that there is always structure and coherence in the intrapreneur's work.

The third and final step is perhaps the most important one: how to attract and retain intrapreneurs. Intrapreneurial leadership must take an honest look at its business practices and make sure that those employees who stand out due to their intrapreneurial qualities are given the chance to grow and are properly recognized for their ideas. Remember that intrapreneurs feel highly identified with your business goals. This is why recognition is essential in order to retain them.

Money is not the only way your company may consider rewarding intrapreneurs. Another important element is to offer them room for creativity. Note the process is effectively and amply used by Google which encourages creativity while increasing productivity: employees are allowed to use 20% of their time in side projects. The results from the 20% time have been extremely positive. The success of such creative license is said to be responsible for Google products such as Gmail, Google Earth, and Gmail labs. As the Google's example shows, giving intrapreneurs creative room is related to their ability to come up with new products and new business opportunities.

Autonomy is also an important aspect that intrapreneurial spirits will require to flourish. It is related to ownership as well as to the ability to circumvent common business processes in order to test new ideas. Forbes' contributor Larry Myler point out that one should combine autonomy with clear and realistic expectations. A good intrapreneur will understand and prefer clear and measurable goals rather than an ambiguous sense of autonomy.

Although they may be open to new ideas and will verbally encouraging innovation, it is often the case that business leaders will fail to accompanying their words with the right actions. Keep in mind that once you have accepted and determined the objectives proposed by your intrapreneurs you cannot hold back on the resources needed to achieve them. Doing so may discourage intrapreneurs and may affect future attempts for them to reach out to you with new ideas for your company to implement.

Intrapreneurs Help Their Parent Companies

"In these troubled, uncertain times, we don't need more command and control; we need better means to engage everyone's intelligence in solving challenges and crises as they arise." ~Dr. Meg Wheatley

Intrapreneurs are employees who show drive in their work, who are fearless when it comes to decision making, and who display complete alignment with a company's goals; intrapreneurs feel strong identification with their company's business objectives. Intrapreneurs are individuals who measure their commitment to a company, based much more than in their perceived monetary rewards alone or at all. Some form of recognition (formal or informal) is key to encouraging intrapreneurs to stay on target, even when there are delays and setbacks.

The personality of intrapreneurs can be summarized in two key elements:

• Successful adaptation of entrepreneurial attitudes and strategies inside of an organization.

• Implementation of start-up practices within a large organization, producing valued innovation.
The question you may be asking at this point is "How can my company identify and take advantage of intrapreneurs?" The answer to this question begins by having a clear understanding of where and how intrapreneurial traits can be best applied within your company. There are five aspects which are the fundamental underpinning of any successful business: innovation, product creation, market share and profits, recruitment and retention of key employees, and perceived levels of job satisfaction.

Intrapreneurs Increase Innovation

"The productivity of a work group seems to depend on how the group members see their own goals in relation to the goals of the organization." ~Dr. Ken Blanchard

An intrapreneurship venture can help your business discover new ideas and harness the creative potential of your employees. Forbes' contributor David Williams declares that keeping intrapreneurs is pivotal for a company that values innovation. Williams maintains that intrapreneurs can trigger innovations within a business, because they think always ahead, which means they spot problems as well as the potential for business opportunities.

Intrapreneurs' shared traits with entrepreneurs make the former a calculative risk taker and someone who is essentially an out-of-the-box thinker. Intrapreneurs have a drive for innovation and experimentation, yet they are not unrealistic in their expectations and their interests. Instead they are individuals who, like entrepreneurs, have a drive for business and for creating products and services that succeed in the market.

If you want to increase your company's ability to innovate intrapreneurs are your best bets. Intrapreneurship will help your company discover new and innovative business opportunities and to unleash your company's creative potential.

Intrapreneurs Unlock Product Creation

"After years of telling corporate citizens to 'trust the system,' many companies must relearn instead to trust their people ~and encourage their people to use neglected creative capacities in order to tap the most potent economic stimulus of all: idea power." ~Rosabeth Moss Kanter

Intrapreneurs possess a key trait for business success and innovation. Business experts refer to this trait as "strategic scanning." This means that intrapreneurs are individuals who are always thinking about what comes next. Intrapreneurs display high levels of engagement and a passionate attitude that is consistent throughout their work relationships. Strategic scanning is essential for businesses to survey and understand the economic environment they face. It allows them to discover shifts in the market as well as new trends.

Next to strategic scanning, intrapreneurs also display highly complex visual thinking. The term "visual thinking" refers to the ability of people to visualize solutions to problems by means of mind maps, figures, and other forms of design thinking. Yet what is so unique to intrapreneurs is that they use such tools in a highly complex manner to always present multiple solutions, possibilities, and strategies.

Strategic scanning and visual thinking are two traits that will highly increase your company's ability to test and create new products; products that attend to unmet needs or which innovate the way people usually conduct processes. In a word, products and services that will most likely assist your business to succeed!

Intrapreneurs should work as pivotal knots within your employee networks. Intrapreneurs can motivate others to adopt a similar attitude and to do so with confidence. The key lies in creating the right environment, where intrapreneurial traits can thrive.

Intrapreneurs Create Higher Profits and Market Share

"Virgin could never have grown into the group of more than 200 companies it is now, were it not for a steady stream of intrapreneurs who looked for and developed opportunities, often leading efforts that went against the grain"
~Sir Richard Branson, Virgin Group

Branson's words are straightforward and to the point. The reason why intrapreneurs are fundamental for your business to increase and sustain its profits is simple: businesses that are able to increase their presence in a market and increase their profits in a sustainable manner are those that are able to take risks, discover new business opportunities, and act decisively to achieve them. This is the reason why business and management scholars maintain that intrapreneurship is especially important in times of recession, when businesses need to discover new business opportunities or need to discover new business processes.

Intrapreneurs will provide your company with the necessary drive and business savvy attitude for new markets to be opened and for new ways of conducting business to be discovered.

Intrapreneurship Make is Possible to Recruit and Retain Key Employees

"I am looking for a lot of people who have an infinite capacity to not know what can't be done." ~Henry Ford

Intrapreneurial traits can also help your business to discover new ways of attracting and keeping talented employees. A particular breed of intrapreneur, which experts refer to as social intrapreneurs, is the type of employee that your company will need for the task. According to Forbes' writer Joseph Agoada social intrapreneurs are those individuals who focus their entrepreneurial capabilities on making change happen. Their role is significant because they can motivate change within a company. *Be the Change You Want to See in your Company*, by Accenture's social intrapreneur Gib Bulloch, is a perfect example of how intrapreneurs can help you keep your employees motivated and engaged.

Intrapreneurs will help your company encourage authenticity, integrity, and humility (this comes from the ancient Aramaic word means teachable, not docile), which intrapreneurs display while at the same time being confident and engaged employees. Intrapreneurs can help your company avoid the overwhelming or overpowering attitude that makes many feel inhibited by promoting and encouraging employee confidence, humility, self-awareness, and purpose.

Intrapreneurship Improves Job Satisfaction

"In the past a leader was a boss. Today's leaders must be partners with their people... they no longer can lead solely based on positional power." ~Dr. Ken Blanchard

In an era marked by the need to enhance collaboration, creativity, and autonomy, intrapreneurs can help you reap the benefits of a more satisfied labor force. Intrapreneurs can help companies build an entrepreneurial culture, which experts point out is a successful business strategy because it leads companies to key innovations and competitive advantages.

"Exemplary leaders know that if they want to gain commitment and achieve the highest standards, they must be models of the behavior they expect of others." ~James M. Kouzes

The Intrapreneurship Paradigm

Intrapreneurs are individuals who can successfully adapt entrepreneurial attitudes and strategies to implement start-up practices within a large organization such as quick decision making, risk taking, and out-of-the-box thinking, which are essential for producing valued innovation.

The benefits for your business come from discovering and taking advantage of new business opportunities, to creating an entrepreneurial environment that encourages employees to be engaged and to take ownership of ambitious initiatives, to increased market share and substantial profit growth.

Identifying, retaining, and attracting intrapreneurs requires the right leadership; bold leaders understand the advantages of nurturing intrapreneurs and will provide them the resources they need to unleash their creative and innovative potential.

Leadership within your organization will need to cultivate and open mind to new, different, our of the norm ideas and become receptive and supportive to "out-of-the-box" thinking.

"Leadership is the capacity to translate vision into reality."
~Warren Bennis

INTRAPRENEURSHIP, IN SOME CASES, WILL BE THE DIFFERENCE BETWEEN CORPORATIONS THAT SURVIVE AND THOSE THAT DO NOT.

INTRAPRENEURSHIP

Chapter 7

3 ENDURING BENEFITS TO EXPECT WHEN INTRAPRENEURSHIP IGNITES WITHIN YOUR ORGANIZATION

"Whenever I see people doing something the way it's always been don, the way it's 'supposed' to be done, that is just a big red flag to me to go look somewhere else." ~Marc Cuban, self-made billionaire and star of Shark Tank

Intrapreneurship Ignites Innovation and Creativity!

A workforce that is universally invested in corporate success and constantly on the lookout for new ways to achieve it cannot help but boost revenue and profit. When a company values their employees and empower them as intrapreneurs, both the intrapreneur and the company benefit. Intrapreneurship has a solid track record of success in product creation and generating more profits! Many experts, in fact, say it may be the best way for established businesses to discover new products and markets and perhaps ensure their very survival in today's rough and tumble corporate world.

- Under 3M's permitted Bootlegging Policy, for example, the Post-it Note, along with many other 3M products, was born.

- Steve Jobs has credited development of the Mac computer to a group of Apple employees who "went back to the garage."

- Ideas pitched by DreamWorks employees, from the creative team to the support staff, have led to such animated blockbusters as Shrek, Madagascar, and Kung Fu Panda.

- Gmail and Google Earth are among the major products that sprang from the ability of Google's workforce to devote 20% of their time to side projects.

- Sony's profitable blockbuster PlayStation product line is an international intrapreneurially created blockbuster success.

- PR1ME Computer grew from a small OTC listed company to become a $480 million sales company (grew 20Xs) in only four years and become the number 1 stock on the NYSE for both sales and profit growth. The intrapreneurially created PR1ME Leasing was a major driving force behind this success.

- Hilton Worldwide Corporation used the intrapreneurial mindset to create a tool to monitor the sustainability of their properties. The tool allowed the corporation to reduce water, energy, carbon outputs, and waste. They saved $147 million through the use of this unique method. They were also able to develop LightStay properties that cater to and qualify for inclusion on sustainable hotel lists.

- Anaconda-Ericsson Inc. utilized the intrapreneurial creation of Anaconda-Ericsson Finance and Leasing Inc. to accelerate and sustain their growth in spite of stiff competition. This new finance division tapped into low SEK Financing (from Swedish Import Export Banks) to structure equipment financing in the Western Hemisphere.

- In the process of globalization corporations ought to think and operate as a younger company. The use of intrapreneurship can create a competitive edge and accelerate organizational change to drive business efforts.

- Once it gains momentum intrapreneurship will help companies grow and expand into new and emerging markets. Companies that are constantly innovating, adapting, and changing to meet customers' needs are typically more successful.

- Organizations can use intrapreneurship effectively and profitably as part of their corporate philosophy to build a culture by having a shared vision. Intrapreneurs are the thinkers and sharers of knowledge and expertise. They are the most likely employees within corporations to share their knowledge, expertise, and to encouraged collaboration.

During the sharing process information is spread on a uniform basis throughout the corporate structure. This process facilitates the spread of the intrapreneurial mindset throughout a company, fostering a culture where all employees in the corporation can voice their ideas and have a responsibility to maintain intrapreneurial values. The result of this process is an employee base that is creative, innovative, and collaborative.

The benefits that employers can expect to see by creating an atmosphere where intrapreneurship not only develops but thrives and eventually bears fruit are many.

Intrapreneurs Create New Products and Services

"What is great about entrepreneurship is that entrepreneurs create the tangible from the intangible." ~Robert Herjavec, self-made Mega Millionaire and star of Shark Tank

With more motivated eyes constantly scouring the horizon for novel and innovative ways to meet the firm's goals the chance of developing a product or service that fills a need or exploits a previously unseen market opportunity expands exponentially. Likewise, discovering entirely new markets and ways to cater to them can also become a regular outcome of the intrapreneurship process. Opportunities that would otherwise never have been seen can be turned into short-term and long-term profit centers.

Intrapreneurship programs allow businesses to develop and test new ideas on a consistent basis. Many companies today rely on innovative and talented individuals within their organizations to think of ideas that have the potential of becoming the next great product or service, though not all of these ideas will be pursued and supported financially.

New and exciting ideas are encouraged from employees as an integral part of the job. Some corporations with successfully structured intrapreneurship programs such as Google allot employees 20% of their time at work to develop new ideas and create innovative projects. They provide their employees the opportunity to participate and engage in innovative practices that potentially makes the company profits in the future.

Companies can utilize intrapreneurship to expand their businesses into new and emerging markets. Companies who have stood the test of time are adaptable and able to change at a relatively fast rate. They are able to create new products and services that allow them to tap into new markets and evolve as time passes with a constant flow. Participating in new markets allows a company to remain competitive and profitable in the long term. It also allows them to grow their profitability and their assets.

Employee Recruitment, Retention, and Satisfaction Grows

"I don't pose as an authority on anything at all, I follow the opinions of the ordinary people I meet, and I take pride in the close-knit teamwork with my organization." ~Walt Disney

The intrapreneurship atmosphere can also improve any business' or organizations' image, making it easier to attract new talent that will push the program even further. If managed aggressively the impacts of a successful intrapreneurship effort can be ongoing and ever expanding. Workers who feel they are a part of an organization that truly values their input and ideas almost always profess far more job satisfaction than those who believe their opinions and suggestions are not taken seriously. Companies that actively encourages individuals to advance ideas and then gives them the tools and the space to develop them create a more contented and productive workplace than one that doesn't.

Forbes contributor, Steve Denning makes this observation, "The survivors in this new world will be those firms whose leaders perceive that the game has changed. A radically different kind of management is required to thrive. It depends on delighting the customer. And this in turn depends on drawing on the full talents and energy of those doing the work. And when people find themselves in situations where they can contribute their full talents and creativity to helping other people, guess what? You have work contexts that create the happiest jobs."

By allowing intrapreneurial employees to stretch themselves through innovative and creative side-projects and showing they will be rewarded for successful efforts, intrapreneurship programs not only make workers happier but also increase their motivation level. Intrapreneurship can create an atmosphere that encourages employees to remain with the organization rather than seek new challenges elsewhere. Considering the high cost of replacing and training new employees, any method that will increase the retention of top workers cannot be undervalued.

Organizations can reach out, entice, effectively recruit the best new employees with an intrapreneurship program that really works. Many recruits look for opportunities to succeed and not only for salary or traditional benefits such as a 401K.

Intrapreneurship can also help build a corporation's or organization's image while recruiting new individuals. A company with a strong intrapreneurship program will attract talented individuals who seek opportunities to work for an establishment that will value their ideas and involve them in the decision making process within the corporate structure. Employees who desire a sense of autonomy and a change in the direction of their careers naturally gravitate toward positions that will give them the opportunity to make profound change both within and outside the corporation.

Profits and Market Share Increase

"Innovation is the specific instrument of entrepreneurship. The act that endows resources with a new capacity to create wealth"
~Peter Drucker.

Intrapreneurship boosts the productivity of employees within any organization, partnership, or a corporation, allowing the business to become more profitable. Allowing employees to be free of excessive control within a corporation allows them to work on their own initiative and shifts the responsibility from centralized corporate control to the employees themselves. The employees become empowered and prior limits and constraints that were imposed by centralized corporate control vanish. The need for another layer of corporate management is eliminated. The employees, as intrapreneurs, have more freedom to brainstorm, operate, and collaborate together. *It is this freedom that is at the core of the intrapreneurial spirit.* The happier the employees are the more productive they are. When they are more productive what naturally follows is an increase in a corporation's profitability.

Intrapreneurs are fundamental for your business to increase and sustain profits. Businesses that are able to increase their market share will increase their profits in a sustained manner. Companies that are able to take risks, discover new business opportunities and act decisively will have higher profits. Intrapreneurship is especially important in times of recession, when businesses need to discover new commerce opportunities or need to discover new business processes. Some of the largest and most successful corporations in the world were created during times of depression or recession because of innovation under fire and the entrepreneurial and intrapreneurial spirit!

Intrapreneurs will provide your company or organization with the necessary drive and business savvy attitude for new markets to be opened, profitable new products and/or services to be created, and for new ways of conducting business to be discovered.

Limiting Potential for Success

"The way we see the problem is the problem." ~Stephen R. Covey

Establishments who do not embrace or encourage the practice of intrapreneurship, in essence, are limiting their own potential for success. They may lose profits due to lack of new products or services and eventually scale down their operations or go out of business. Companies that cannot adapt or change in a timely manner often do not survive and may go out of business.

One recent and unfortunate example of this is Blockbuster. Blockbuster video lost much of its profits, closed most of its brick and mortar stores, and went bankrupt because it failed to break into the internet streaming market quickly enough. As a result, Netflix, their competition, dominated this market as video rentals shifted to streaming movies and videos from the World Wide Web.

Another example that comes to mind is Borders. Borders bookseller failed to tap into the eBook market as opposed to other companies such as Apple, Amazon.com, Barnes and Noble, and Sony who transitioned into selling electronic books online. Borders completely went out of business and closed all of their failing brick and mortar stores.

These are two examples of companies that fell on hard times financially as a result of a lack of innovation and forward thinking.

"Logic will get you from A to B. Imagination will take you everywhere." ~Albert Einstein

CORPORATIONS WHO TAP INTO NEW MARKETS IN AN EMERGING ECONOMY CAN ATTRACT THOUSANDS OR SOMETIMES MILLIONS OF NEW CUSTOMERS.

Chapter 8

6 KEY WAYS TO BUILD A CULTURE OF INTRAPRENEURSHIP

"We grow great by dreams. All big men are dreamers. They see things in the soft haze of a spring day or in the red fire of a long winter's evening. Some of us let these great dreams die, but others nourish and protect them; nurse them through bad days till they bring them to the sunshine and light which comes always to those who sincerely hope that their dreams will come true."
~Woodrow Wilson

Ignite Innovation!

The process of intrapreneurship generally results in a much more satisfied and productive workforce for these and other intrapreneurial proponents. Why? Employees in such organizations are empowered to nurture their most creative impulses in an atmosphere that is both open and supportive. Intrapreneurial employees are recognized and rewarded when they succeed and not be personally punished for project setbacks, delays, or failures.

Companies that foster such behavior were founded on a culture of innovation and calculated risk-taking and are therefore willing to look beyond any short-term disruptions that may occur when employees are regularly focused on projects of their own making.

ANY COMPANY THAT REALLY WANTS TO CAN BUILD A SUCCESSFUL INTRAPRENEURSHIP PROGRAM AND ULTIMATELY REAP THE REWARDS!

1) Show you mean business

Employees will be more apt to dive into the process of intrapreneurship, which can certainly be intimidating at the outset, when they know the company is serious about it. The concept must be truly embedded into an organization's core practices and tied directly to its goals. Many firms formalize the process further by appointing someone with a title such as Chief Innovation Officer, and then giving that person the power to truly be the sparkplug for the effort.

2) Include your entire organization

Even if an intrapreneurship program is formalized and an enthusiastic go-to manager is appointed, these efforts will rarely succeed if they are perceived as being aimed at only a few elite individuals or a select group of departments. To truly create widespread innovation, the behavior must be encouraged across the whole company. The best efforts also nurture cross-discipline collaborations, and sometimes external networking.

3) Seek out the intrapreneurs already there

Organizations will discover that they don't have to search far to find creative and innovative workers already in their employ. They simply must identify those that exist and then enlist them in the development of their program. Employers should also give these budding intrapreneurs sufficient room to pursue their interests, and keep others in the organization consistently aware of their actions and progress when appropriate. Finally, these employees should be encouraged to recruit peers into their programs and suggest to others where they could proceed on their own.

4) Make time for innovation and creativity

Many intrapreneurship program proponents have found success by designating specific time, or percentage of their time, off from regular responsibilities when employees can pursue these activities. This works because employees can focus entirely on their day jobs most of the time, and then focus completely on these efforts at predictable intervals. Google lets employees spend up to 20 % of their workweek on side projects. LinkedIn offers uninterrupted 30 to 90 day blocks of time for intrapreneurship.

5) Actively promote the activities

Actively publicizing ongoing intrapreneurial efforts throughout the organization on a regular basis demonstrates real support and can help generate additional ideas. Add to the transparency and demonstrated organizational support by clearly showing how these efforts advance the mission and goals of the company. Always give credit where credit is due and allow intrapreneurship leaders to take ownership of their projects.

6) Make failure acceptable and reward success

Risk-taking is a critical part of the process, yet for a number of reasons a corporate intrapreneur may tend to be more cautious than a solo entrepreneur. Because of this it is particularly important to let everyone know management recognizes that failure is a part of the process, and mean it. Consequently, when real success is achieved it should be celebrated across the organization and recognized financially or in some other way whenever possible.

"Develop success from failures. Discouragement and failure are two steps of the surest stepping stones to success."
~Dale Carnegie

SMART ORGANIZATIONS RECOGNIZE THAT NURTURING INTRAPRENEURSHIP WILL BE BENEFICIAL FOR THEIR ORGANIZATIONAL HEALTH AS WELL AS THEIR BOTTOM LINE. IT TAKES SOME EFFORT TO DEVELOP PROPERLY, BUT THE RESULTS SPEAK FOR THEMSELVES.

Chapter 9

10 EFFECTIVE WAYS TO ENCOURAGE INNOVATION, RISK TAKING, AND OUT-OF-THE-BOX THINKING, STARTING TODAY!

"Dreamers are mocked as impractical. The truth is they are the most practical, as their innovations lead to progress and a better way of life for all of us." ~Robin S. Sharma

The Competitive Advantage of Intrapreneurship

The use of intrapreneurship can be vastly successful in boosting a company's bottom line when the approach is fully integrated into the corporate structure and becomes part of its core business practices. Employees who are allowed to think and act as intrapreneurs will do so.

Executives who stand in solid support of their intrapreneurs enjoy a substantial return on their investments and are rewarded by capitalizing on new product lines and services that are profitable in both the short-term and long-term.

Intrapreneurship can produce impressive results in innovation, product creation, and procedural development. A company that realizes such gains is one that truly supports its employees as they work to turn their innovative ideas into plans for action. It is one that gives people the space they need to take some risks in the pursuit of these projects. And it is one that encourages this out-of-the-box thinking in all corners of the organization.

It might be easier to launch a new idea when backed by a corporation but an intrapreneurial idea still involves a lot of hard work. Remember some employees may burn the midnight oil as they juggle their regular responsibilities with intrapreneurial ventures.

An intrapreneurial effort can be intimidating even though it is officially encouraged and no personal capital is involved. There is still often fear about job security being threatened by failure. Make sure people are not afraid to fail.

Secrets of a Successful Intrapreneurship Program
"Keep in mind that imagination is at the heart of all innovation. Crush or constrain it and the fun will vanish."
~Albert-László Barabási

1. Get middle and senior management on board

Senior management will have approved the intrapreneurship program and the general work force will likely be its most active participants. The level between, however, must also buy in to the importance and opportunities of a successful intrapreneurship program in order to make the effort successful over the long haul. Middle managers just might come up with some of the best ideas of all.

2. Make the organization's goals and strategies visible to all

An organization should encourage better solutions to meet different requirements or existing market needs. Intrapreneurship cannot successfully be conducted in the dark.

3. Promote and Publicize ongoing efforts

A co-worker who hears about an idea under development may provide the "missing link" that brings it to fruition. This is exactly how the final touches were put on the work-in-progress that became the Post-it Note (3M) and the Elixir Guitar String Line (W. L. Gore) which resulted in intrapreneurial success.

4. Encourage employees from different departments to work together.

Constantly challenge the workforce to come up with new ideas for products and services and repeatedly encourage them to look beyond their own defined circles of responsibility for ways to make them happen. The interchanging of ideas and input are beneficial to the intrapreneurial process.

5. Offer speakers and classes on creative thinking.

Bring employees together with experts, speakers, and professors to learn new ways that they might better put knowledge of their business and industry and their imaginations to intrapreneurial work.

6. Provide easy ways for employees to sound out ideas.

A section on the company intranet or an idea suggestion box in the break room for submission of ideas can be useful for soliciting prospective projects that might only need the right feedback to turn them into successful products or services.

7. Make company assets and resources available for intrapreneurial success.

The biggest advantage intrapreneurs have over entrepreneurs is access to their company's financial, technological, production, and marketing resources. Make sure that development support is available whenever possible.

8. Set milestones and reporting paths.

Participants must understand that all reasonable intrapreneurial efforts have to move along without, of course, negatively impacting their regular company duties. Keep people on track and keep their ideas from dwindling.

9. Keep recognition flowing.

Praise and recognition can go a long way and its impact can never be understated in the intrapreneurship process.

10. Make the intrapreneurship process enjoyable.

Jerry Greenfield, one of the Co-Founders of the iconic Ben & Jerry's, once famously said, "If it's not fun, why do it?" No one can deny that this attitude helped his small Vermont creamery innovate its way into becoming one of the most successful and best-known names in the food business.

The most important asset to any organization is the collective intellect and experience of the employees who are employed by the company. Smart companies recognize talented individuals and will hand-pick these promising key employees, educate them, invest in their ideas, and offer them their full support. These corporations and organizations understand that in order to keep productivity and capacity for innovation high their intrapreneurs need to be satisfied in their work efforts. Their intrapreneurs need all the tools, resources, and support they can get to successfully create and operate their ventures. Enlightened organizations ensure that their employees are equipped with whatever they need to be successful.

"Most of us understand that innovation is enormously important. It's the only insurance against irrelevance. It's the only guarantee of long-term customer loyalty. It's the only strategy for out-performing a dismal economy." ~*Gary Hamel*

Innovation is a catalyst for growth. Innovation allows corporations to grow their assets and profits. They may use the profits they generate to expand their operations, open new divisions, or acquire other companies.

Corporations who strategically grow their businesses are frequently diversifying their product offerings and tapping into new markets. To tap into new and emerging markets effectively corporations must constantly improve already existing products or offer new and different products to their customer base. New products and services allow corporations to keep their existing customers and also expand their customer base by consistently adding new members to it.

INNOVATION, SOMETIMES REFERRED TO AS THINKING OUT-OF-THE-BOX, REFERS TO RENEWING, CHANGING, OR CREATING MORE EFFECTIVE PROCESSES, PRODUCTS, SERVICES, TECHNOLOGIES, IDEAS, OR WAYS OF DOING THINGS. IN ORDER TO BE INNOVATIVE, EMPLOYEES MUST HAVE A SUPPORTIVE ENVIRONMENT WHERE THEY CAN BE CREATIVE.

Chapter 10

HOW TO OPERATE A SUCCESSFUL INTRAPRENEURSHIP PROGRAM

"Two people can see the same thing, disagree, and yet both be right. It's not logical; it's psychological." ~Stephen R. Covey

Embrace a New Way of Thinking

In order to create an intrapreneurship program, organizations, corporations, partnerships, and non-profits must learn how to be adaptable and deal with systemic change. Important changes need to be made within the corporate structure for intrapreneurship to thrive. Successful intrapreneurship programs allow a degree of freedom to be enjoyed by the organizations' employees.

Enlightened organizations recognize that the old "command and control" managerial style is no longer effective. There organizations understand that in order to become a true trail blazer or maverick means sometimes ignoring the rules or breaking the rules to get things done. In response to this many corporations have to relax company policies and rules in order to facilitate intrapreneur's efforts within new divisions to operate with less red tape.

Organizational bureaucracy has been innovation's major obstacle. Barriers act to slow the process of innovation making it more time consuming and more frustrating to create a viable new product or service.

For innovation to occur unimpeded all stumbling blocks that may jeopardize or hamper the process from running smoothly must be removed. The only way to do this effectively is for a corporation to change their system of operations. In other words, change rules and policies to support intrapreneurs.

Sir Richard Branson, founder of the Virgin Group, candidly suggests that businesses should empower their employees to break the rules. He views intrapreneurs as not having to follow company routines or protocols. He states that the Virgin Group would have never grown and expanded into 200 companies if it was not for intrapreneurs. These are individuals that seek out opportunities and develop opportunities that may go against the grain. He recalls one clear example of this. One of his young designers took up the challenge to solve design problems that were plaguing Virgin Atlantic's upper class cabin. He was able to design herring bone suites for sleeping and made millions of their customers very happy. No large design firms proposed any viable solutions. By enabling this young designer to pursue his vision Virgin Atlantic was able to solve a problem in a relatively short time resulting in one of the first airlines to boast sleeper suites within an airplane.

"Vision without action is a daydream. Action with without vision is a nightmare." ~Japanese Proverb

Many organizations and corporations realize that from time to time they must re-invent themselves in order to stay at the forefront of business and navigate into new, unchartered waters. They must change the direction in which they are going to expose themselves to new opportunities. Profound change occurs over a period of time. For corporations to stay competitive in a changing global economy they must change and evolve. A corporation that stays static typically has a small variety of products or services to offer their clientele. This approach to business only works in a small amount of niche markets. In a global economy however organizations must be able to offer their clientele many new and different products and services. They must constantly innovate and stay one step ahead of their competition if they expect to survive. In order to generate and test new ideas corporations need to have a formal intrapreneurship program in place.

Intrapreneurship is a process, not an event. Working independently, but with official sanction, individuals within an organization that promotes intrapreneurship are able to turn their innovative ideas into hot new products and services. Organizations that implement intrapreneurship properly and promote it aggressively are the ones that will reap the most rewards.

Reap Rewards: Strategies for Companies

"The best way to predict the future is to create it." ~Peter Drucker

- Set goals and be open to new strategies of innovation. Create a vision of what the top executives desire the program to achieve. Intrapreneurs have a higher than average intelligence, are goal oriented, and combine action and vision. Provide resources and all that is required to help an intrapreneur move progressively through the learning curve.

- Offer intrapreneurship training. Invite the most motivated and energetic employees to take part in the training. It will be easy to recognize those that are in synch with the company's vision and want the opportunity to make a beneficial difference while desiring to climb the corporate ladder. Have policies in place that will allow time for intrapreneurs to learn more about the corporation and the various divisions within the industry.

- Appoint a senior point person to oversee everything and give them the authority to make good things happen. An intrapreneurship program will never meet its potential unless the organization that launches it is really committed to making it work. Tie the program directly to relevant company strategies and goals and make sure everyone knows it.

- Let go of rigid practices that no longer work. There is too much competition out there to not be willing to be more pioneering innovative and creative.

- Foster innovation. There are two types of innovation, incremental and radical. Incremental innovation utilizes a well-designed system for evolution of the product or services into new market areas. Radical innovation utilizes a more drastic approach that radically transforms the corporation. This approach requires experimentation to find what works and what doesn't. This is more difficult to manage because it requires constant determined vision.

- Allow for delays, set-backs, and failure in the intrapreneurship program. It takes time and practice for the system to get into full gear. Encouragement is required in order to keep the intrapreneurial team motivated.

- Keep the company's hierarchy and bureaucracy from becoming a stumbling block. Well before the program is launched; ensure that all executives and middle managers truly buy into the effort by helping them fully understand its scope and potential upside. Additionally, be willing to ease or perhaps suspend any existing organizational rules, processes, procedures, or customs that could stymie its optimal implementation. All layers of management within an organization, senior and middle managers must provide their full support to ensure their organization's future success. Managers must be willing to empower, be open, and give their intrapreneurs freedom to do what is necessary to achieve their goals.

- Provide existing company resources to intrapreneurial participants and their teams. One of the big advantages that intrapreneurs have over entrepreneurs is the organizational support their employment can provide. The in-house technological, marketing, and production expertise already available can often make the difference between an idea being successfully advanced or unceremoniously abandoned.

- Create a special grant program or venture capital pool. Some ideas need a bit of financial support as well as technical expertise, and this is a good way to provide targeted fiscal resources to qualified participants. Require applicants to submit detailed business and action plans and a set of accountability benchmarks can also help ensure the funds are dispersed to intrapreneurial proposals that have the best chance to succeed.

- Spark new ideas. Get the entire organization excited and involved. Make certain that personnel throughout the company, no matter their department, level, or responsibility, know about the program and understand they are included in it. Increase enthusiasm by scheduling brown bag lunches or other gatherings that highlight innovation, creativity and out-of-the-box thinking.

- Identify known innovators and help nurture and support their passion and creativity. Employers can usually pick out the best and the brightest in their midst and should focus from the start on bringing them into active intrapreneurial roles. Encouraging them to identify and mentor other future leaders can also pay big dividends in the long term.

- Allow lead participants to assemble their dream teams. This promotes a setting for brainstorming and implementation. These teams will work semi-autonomously to create new ideas. Give these people the leeway to approach and bring on board anyone in the organization that they believe they need to succeed. Encourage intrapreneurs to recruit from other departments in order to bring additional qualities, complementary skills and new perspectives into the process.

- Observe and identify potential intrapreneurs that may already be employed by the corporation. Those employees that exhibit the characteristics of leadership and innovative tendencies are the life-blood of the corporation. Tap into their talents, abilities, and creativity.

- Allocate employees time to be innovative and to think outside-the-box. Better yet, get rid of the box. When companies display their real commitment to these efforts they often get maximum results by allowing these side projects to be pursued during the regular work day. This can be accomplished with a set number of hours per week allocated to such efforts, or with a longer single period of concentrated time. The important thing is to determine the parameters of the time and make it available.

- Dedicate employees space to innovative. It is absolutely critical that everyone understands intrapreneurial efforts involve a lengthy series of trial and error, and a failure or two along the way is both unavoidable and acceptable. Risk-taking is a key part of the intrapreneurial process and everyone has to know that management recognizes this and won't penalize intrapreneurs for stepping out on a limb or for setbacks.

- Establish a formal communication process so management and all participants will remain consistently on the same page. Don't allow individual efforts to lag; inertia is the death of innovation. Combat it by requiring accountability with clearly defined benchmarks and metrics as a condition for continued organizational support.

- Recognize solid work and reward success in your company's intrapreneurial activities and ventures. Have a system in place for recognition and rewards to encourage and support innovation. Consistently publicizing ongoing efforts at company meetings and through internal publications and financially rewarding those projects that really do pan out provide at least two significant benefits. For one, participants see that their work is appreciated and they become even more motivated to press on. For another, the enthusiasm this spawns is contagious and some potential stars that have yet to participate may join in.

Successful organizations and corporations have formal intrapreneurship programs that empower their employees to drive innovation. The end result of innovation is corporate viability and profitability. A corporation that is viable and profitable creates new products, services, and solutions on a continual basis that strengthen the organization's bottom line. New products, services, and solutions generate new clients and new opportunities for earning profits.

"The empires of the future are empires of the mind."
~Winston Churchill

Sir Richard Branson mentions that he created the intrapreneur position within the Virgin Group to enable carefully selected employees, who have the knowledge and the experience, help guide the corporation in business ventures that are unfamiliar, such as mobile phones. The corporation had no prior experience operating a mobile phone company. They hired the best managers in the industry, enticing them away from their competition. They were willing to offer these individuals freedom as intrapreneurs and encouraged them to establish companies within the Virgin Group. He stresses that intrapreneurs "know which end is up."

Intrapreneurs must be given the freedom to build meaningful relationships and collaborate effectively with other employees and with corporate management personnel. In an effort to obtain the resources they need to create and test their projects they must be effective communicators and be able to ask key personnel for resources. Whether it is knowledge, material goods, financial assistance, time, or extra employees to assist intrapreneurs, these resources are crucial forms of support given to employees who participate in successful intrapreneur programs. They are given whatever assistance is needed to transform a project into a successful venture.

INTRAPRENEURSHIP IS A PROCESS. SUCCESSFUL ORGANIZATIONS, PARTNERSHIPS, NON-PROFITS, AND CORPORATIONS THAT HAVE FORMAL INTRAPRENEURSHIP PROGRAMS WHICH EMPOWER THEIR EMPLOYEES TO DRIVE INNOVATION ARE ABLE TO TURN THEIR GROUND-BREAKING IDEAS INTO HOT NEW PRODUCTS AND SERVICES.

THE END RESULT OF INNOVATION IS ORGANIZATIONAL VIABILITY AND PROFITABILITY.

iNTRAPRENEURSHIP

Chapter 11

Intrapreneurial Case Studies

Apple Macintosh

"Innovation has nothing to do with how many R&D dollars you have. When Apple came up with the Mac, IBM was spending at least 100 times more on R&D. It's not about money. It's about the people you have, how you're led, and how much you get it."
~Steve Jobs

The Apple Macintosh is a line of personal computers. The project for its creation began in 1976 when an Apple employee, Jef Raskin, had a vision of a low-cost computer for the average consumer that was easy to use. Jef presented his idea to Steve Jobs and had wanted to name the project McIntosh, after his favorite Apple. Due to legalities, the name had to be changed. Phonetically, it was too close to the manufacturer of the McIntosh audio equipment. Steve Jobs had attempted to persuade the manufacturer to release the name, but his request was denied. Jobs ended up purchasing the rights to use the name. Jobs still kept the product name Apple Macintosh.

The creation of the Macintosh computer was a successful milestone at Apple as the popularity of the machine was at its peak throughout the decade. "Develop a completely different class of users" was the key intention of Apple. Considering this issue Steve Jobs put most of his talents on the production/manufacturing line. Steve Jobs is well known for popularizing the intrapreneurship terminology. He had picked 20 of his best Apple engineers to work on this project. Under the leadership of Jobs the team worked completely independently from anyone else at Apple. One of the most popular news comments made was that Jobs and his Band of Engineers were playing "without adult supervision." Jobs fully intended for the products created by this group to become competitive with other Apple products.

Jef Raskin was given the authorization to begin hiring people to work together as an independent intrapreneurial team on the project. He first began to search for an engineer who could create a prototype of his vision. There was already an existing team within Apple that was working on another project. That team's name was Lisa. The engineer associated with that team was Bill Atkinson. Atkinson introduced Raskin to another engineer, Burrell Smith, who was self-taught and had been working at the company as a service technician for approximately a year.

Raskin had interviewed quite a few people and several years later eventually assembled a large team that developed and created the original version of Macintosh software. Burrell Smith built the first version according to Jef Raskin's specifications. It consisted of 64 kilobytes and utilized the Motorola 6809E microprocessor and the display was in black and white.

A member of the Lisa team, Bud Tribble thought it might be interesting to see if the graphical programs they had created would run on the Macintosh. He approached Raskin and asked if he could try something. He asked if he could run Lisa's Motorola 68000 microprocessor in the Macintosh and explained it would still help to keep the cost of production down. By the end of 1980 Tribble had successfully generated a board that worked with the better processor and also increased the speed from 5 MHz to 8 MHz's Since this version used less RAM chips, the production cost was even lower. The final MAC self-contained design evolved through the years to a new MAC in 1998. Work went on as enhancements and improvements continued to be generated.

Apple made its announcement regarding migration to Intel in 2005 at the World Wide Developers Conference (WWDC). Apple also discontinued the microprocessor known as 'Power PC' in 2006, immediately after the WWDC. That also changed the hardware aspect of Macintosh. Since then, all Mac machines have been developed using Intel's x86 processors.

Macintosh first competed with both Microsoft and Intel during the mid-1990s. Intel's Pentium processor, along with Microsoft's Windows 95 OS, significantly improved both GUI (Graphical User Interface) and multimedia capability compared with Macintosh. Apple tried their best to stay on top of Microsoft and Intel by enhancing the operating system of Mac and introduced virtual memory and co-operative multitasking.

Apple also established 'Apple Industrial Design Group', in order to bring a new look and shape to all Apple products including Macintosh. Unfortunately not all of Apple's efforts worked out effectively and a large portion of computer users had started using Microsoft's OS on Intel's machine (processor). With Steve Jobs back on-board Apple began developing new business strategies after projecting the scope and possibilities of next generation computing. Instead of pushing only the Macintosh in the market, Apple made investments in smart phones and other mini-multimedia devices. All Apple products were renamed as iProducts, and Macintosh has been known as the iMac since then.

Apple increased its business again with a completely new set of product lines including the iMac, iPhone, iPad, and iPod. Recent years have brought Apple to a unique and different tech brand with thousands of loyal consumers. Apple also brought Intel's new I/O interface, which was known as Thunderbolt, in the market.

Apple's iMac is now occupying around 32.9% of the PC market; particularly all-in-one PCs. Apple currently has a 33% market share.

The 4th Quarter of 2014 proved the growth for the company is its iMac desktops. Apple sold 5.52 million units during the quarter, which comes to a 21% increase from the same period a year ago. This represents the highest jump in iMac sales since December 2011, and Apple seems poised to exploit the healthy iMac segment for the foreseeable future.

Through intrapreneurship and Steve Jobs a highly successful marketable product was created and continues to flourish today. Steve Jobs encouraged intrapreneurship and knew that the members of the team had to be innovative, willing to take risks, and focused on the mission to the point of being willing to lose their jobs to defend the program itself.

Adobe Systems

"Learning and innovation go hand in hand. The arrogance of success is to think that what you did yesterday will be sufficient for tomorrow" ~William Pollard

Intrapreneurs are used by companies to cultivate new and innovative ideas that will become profitable ventures in the future. Adobe Systems is a trailblazer in this area. They have recognized and accepted that the survival of their company now and in the future depends on offering their customers and clients products they want and need. In response to this, Adobe Systems has nurtured the practice of allowing key employees to research and develop solutions that will fit the needs of their customers. This management style that integrates innovation and risk taking is becoming more of a necessity in today's corporate world.

Erik Larson of Adobe Systems hosts a blog called Intrapreneurship 2.0. In this blog Erik discusses the idea of the "digital customer experience." He points out that over the next ten years there will be a huge shift or change in the way businesses operate on the internet. He emphasizes that what is important is being aware of the expectations of consumers and how their expectations will change and evolve over a period of time.

Larson reveals the philosophy of Adobe Systems' use of intrapreneurship. He states that intrapreneurs take advantage of technology and resources within their organization to change the business and digital experience. Large organizations such as Adobe think about ROI (return on investment) all the time. He stresses that if a company is to going to spend $50 million, then saving 10% means something. Intrapreneurs must actively manage risk because they have a lot to lose. They are responsible to the people that matter. He mentions that Adobe Systems focuses on their existing customers. They understand that investing in the way one does business can have a major return in the long run.

Adobe Systems also recognizes that fixing business processes matters because it impacts all the different customers they have.

In terms of the customer experience laying a foundation for the next wave of innovation is crucial. Adobe is focused on customer-centric problems that may arise in the future. This results from figuring out what the customer wants and delivering it in a digital experience. The most important piece is designing from customers in and not from systems out. They believe one must invest in the design upfront before beginning a project.

Succeeding in business is finding out what your customer expects and then meeting their expectations. Customers' expectations for digital experiences such as use of a website are determined by products they are already using and which are convenient such as Google, Amazon.com, and Facebook. Customers also look for digital experiences to be available at any time, to be engaging and interesting, and to be authentic.

3M (Minnesota, Mining, and Manufacturing)

"Listen to anyone with an original idea, no matter how absurd it may sound at first. If you put fences around people, you get sheep. Give people the room they need."
~William McKnight, 3M President

Post-it Notes

3M Corporation was able to capitalize on the creative idea of intrapreneurs Spencer Silver and Art Fry to create and launch the 3M Post-it Note product. 3M chemical scientist Spencer Silver invented a not-so-sticky adhesive in 1968 but it took him several years to come up with how to best use and market the product. Spencer shared his idea through seminars in which he shared the features (and benefits) of this semi-adhesive to fellow 3M employees.

"It was part of my job as a researcher to develop new adhesives, and at that time we wanted to develop bigger, stronger, tougher adhesives. This was none of those." ~Spencer Silver, 3M

For five long years no one really caught the vision of his product until a co-worker, Art Fry, recognized the need for Spencer's idea. During choir practice and performances Fry's bookmarks were regularly falling out of his hymn book. This product concept solved his problem! It took another decade however until, in 1980, 3M's Post-it Notes product line was successfully launched across the entire US and internationally.

"I got to known as 'Mr. Persistent,' because I wouldn't give up!"
~Spencer Silver, 3M

Intrapreneurial Grants

3M regularly awards 15 grants for intrapreneurially created products each year by their employee ~intrapreneur teams. 3M is proud to point out their intrapreneurship program's success in increasing innovation and the profitable creation of many products in addition to 3M Post-It Notes®. If an intrapreneurial idea is considered as a potentially viable product then 3M funds the product through the 3M program called the Genesis Grant. The grant offers intrapreneurs up to $85,000 to guide their innovative projects past the idea stage.

3M has a formal panel of technical experts and scientists who initially review ideas that a 3M intrapreneur has submitted. If a project passes the initial panels review then it is sent to another committee of senior technical, marketing, and management experts.

The second review panel specifically looks for creative ideas that may lead to a competitive advantage in a specific market segment. This panel carefully reviews projects where some preliminary experimental work has already been completed and data is available to analyze. This panel identifies what resources may be required from both within and outside 3M for the intrapreneurially created projects.

Additional products that have resulted from 3M's intrapreneurship program includes the 3M multilayer optical film technology, 3M's Vikuiti™, and 3M Scotch® Pop-Up Tape.

DreamWorks Animation

"I don't dream at night, I dream all day; I dream for a living."
~Steven Spielberg, DreamWorks Animation

DreamWorks Animation, a successful animation studio in Glendale, California, once a "spin-off" of DreamWorks Studios, has established itself as its own company through the intrapreneurial efforts of CEO Jeff Katzenberg. DreamWorks Animation creates, produces, and engages in the distribution of digital media such as feature films, television programs, and video games. Most of its films are marketed and distributed under the Touchstone label that Walt Disney Studios owns.

DreamWorks Studios was established in 1994 for Steven Spielberg, David Geffen, and Jeffrey Katzenberg. Collectively the three founders owned 72% of the company. Microsoft's co-founder Paul Allen owned the rest. The successful sitcom *Spin City* was the first venture embarked on by the studio. Its first feature film was *The Peacemaker* released in September 1997. Their follow-up release, *Amistad,* was Steven Spielberg's first film with the company. *Amistad* was nominated for four Academy Awards.

In 1998 Steven Spielberg released *Saving Private Ryan*. The film was the highest grossing film of 1998. Of the 11 academy awards it was nominated for it won 5. Spielberg won Best Director for the film. The first two animated feature films created by the studio, *Antz* and *The Prince of Egypt*, were also released in 1998. Antz was the first computer generated feature film produced by DreamWorks. *The Prince of Egypt* was created using traditional and computer generated animation.

In 2000 DreamWorks Animation created the computer generated feature film *Shrek* featuring the talents of Mike Meyers, Eddie Murphy, and Cameron Diaz. It won an Academy Award for Best Animated Feature Film. The sequel to *Shrek*, *Shrek 2*, was released in 2004. Headed by founder Jeffrey Katzenberg DreamWorks then established a new animation division dedicated to producing computer generated (CGI) animated films named

DreamWorks Animation. In 2000 DreamWorks acquired Pacific Data Images, LLC (PDI), restructuring the facility into its present Northern California animation division in Redwood City, CA.

Katzenberg, a former chairman of Disney, is no stranger to leading a successful animation company. Applying his entrepreneurial expertise he has nurtured DreamWorks Animation into the successful global entertainment leader it is today. Under his leadership DreamWorks Animation has created and released a total of 27 feature films. Some of their most successful and top-grossing intrapreneurially created animated films include *Shrek*, *Madagascar, Kung Fu Panda, How to Train Your Dragon*, and *Monsters vs. Aliens.*

Jeffrey Katzenberg has stated that, "At the heart of DreamWorks Animation is the desire to tell great stories and inspire audiences. Our company culture not only encourages employees to create but also to innovate and ultimately have fun! We have transformed over the years from hand-drawn animation to computer-generated films to being a leader in 3D entertainment. Our strategy has remained the same; to produce great stories that are creatively driven and technologically state of the art. In pursuit of this goal, I'm proud to say that what defines DreamWorks Animation more than anything else is the dedication and the expertise of our people."

As CEO Katzenberg recognizes how important his employees and intrapreneurship are to the success of his company as a whole. It is the intrapreneurial efforts of his dedicated staff that ultimately inspires and entertains audiences around the world. He fully supports a company culture that encourages employees to be creative and to innovate. He also acknowledges that great stories are both creatively and technologically driven. Their finished products are unique, state of the art, animated films that bring a great story to life. These are stories that appeal to both children and adults alike. They are experiences that can be shared and enjoyed by the whole family.

DreamWorks Animation encourages intrapreneurial values by formally teaching classes to their employees on creating and selling their ideas to others. Jeffrey Katzenberg understands that successful intrapreneurs must know how to sell their ideas. The company specifically trains their employees to present their ideas to executives for creative input from ideas for a new movie to novel food choices for their cafeteria.

The key to staying competitive and maintaining profitability is building a strong intrapreneurial culture within the corporate structure. New products and customer experiences are created through the innovation and intrapreneurial ideas of their talented employees. It is these key individuals that are the creative engines that "drive" the corporation into new and emerging markets. The more individuals a company can successfully teach and train the more innovation occurs producing new products and services and the more profitable a corporation will be now and in the future.

In 2006 DreamWorks Studio sold DreamWorks to the Viacom Corporation, a parent company of Paramount Pictures. Then in 2008, DreamWorks (consisting of partners Steven Spielberg and Stacy Snider) ended its partnership with Paramount Studios and partnered with Reliance Anil Dhirubhai Ambani Group to produce its films. This group also provided the capital to DreamWorks to operate as an independent entity.

"Dreams are extremely important. You can't do it unless you imagine it." ~George Lucas (Dream Works)

Google

"We don't have a traditional strategy process, planning process like you'd find in traditional technical companies. It allows Google to innovate very, very quickly, which I think is a real strength of the company." ~Eric Schmidt, Executive Chairman, Google

Google has been successful developing and implementing several unique intrapreneurial programs and business models such as the 20% Innovation Time Off program, Entrepreneur in Residence, and Startup Incubators to recruit and keep talented individuals. Google continues to be a leader in the world of innovation and a pioneer in intrapreneurship.

20% Innovation Time-Off Program

The corporation has developed and implemented a formal process known as 20% Innovation Time Off. Google realized that their key employees already involved in innovative projects needed time to create future products and services. Through the Innovation Time Off program, Google allows their employees freedom to spend up to 20% of their time at work to pursue projects they think will benefit the corporation. The intrapreneurship program has been highly successful and has created many e products such as Gmail, Google News, AdSense, Orkut, Google Earth, and Google Apps.

The intrapreneurship program at Google gives employees the opportunity to develop ideas that they can bring to fruition. With this powerful strategy, Google ensures and maintains a constant flow of products and services that will allow the corporation to grow, stay competitive, and ensure their survival.

Intrapreneurs are required to write and submit a proposal and a timeline for their project. They state how it is they will monitor, measure, and evaluate the success of their project. Corporate executives consider all submitted proposals and support the ventures they think will be most profitable in the future.

The intrapreneur program at Google increases employee satisfaction by allowing their employees' ideas to be acknowledged and rewarded.

Entrepreneur-in-Residence

Google has created a formal role called Entrepreneur In Residence (EIR) or Chief Innovation Officer for proven intrapreneurs within their corporation. They developed this position to stay ahead of the curve and have also appointed these talented individuals to consult with them on startups.

Stacy Brown-Philpot joined the Google Ventures team as an EIR. She advised the Google's portfolio companies in business and consumer technology, mobile, payment, and marketplace divisions. Her business experience includes 10 years leading operations on a global scale for Google Search, Google Chrome, and Google+. Google rewarded her and promoted her to several senior positions in finance as a result of her experience and her talent as an intrapreneur. She was responsible for managing revenue for the corporation, implementing operations to enhance the customer experience, and developing practical solution methods for payments. Her philosophy on management is making changes and being a continual learner. She emphasizes that to make changes she needed to change positions at Google several times. Each new experience allowed her to learn new things about business. To stay current innovators must be lifelong learners.

Google's Startup Incubator in San Francisco

Google encourages intrapreneurship within the company through the establishment of startup incubators headed by intrapreneurs who have proved to be innovative and responsible. John Hanke, an intrapreneur who led Google Maps, was appointed to head a new startup incubator in San Francisco. The corporation rewarded John with the opportunity to manage his own division and team members. His team of about 20 employees worked on social networking, mobile, and location based apps.

Through this strategy Google has been able to keep talented individuals from acquired companies for a longer period of time. They have a great track record for keeping these key employees. The benefit of keeping this talent is that they have past success with creating new products and services, making good decisions, managing resources, and demonstrating initiative and leadership skills. They would also know how to inspire, motivate, and coach other intrapreneurs effectively.

Google is a trailblazer in the world of intrapreneurship and remains at the cutting edge of innovation. Google's intrapreneurial strategies such as the 20% Innovation Time Off program, Entrepreneur in Residence, and Startup Incubators have been successful in providing a mechanism through which the corporation can grow in new areas and thrive. These techniques have helped the organization sustain profits and ensure future profits with an influx of products and services on a consistent basis.

In her June 30, 2006 seminar at Stanford University, Marissa Mayer, Google's then Vice President of Search Products and User Experience at that time, revealed that half of all new product launches had originated from the Google intrapreneurship program: Innovation Time Off. Marissa is now President and CEO of Yahoo!

PR1ME Computer

"A dream doesn't become reality through magic; it takes sweat, determination and hard work."- Colin Powell

PR1ME Computer, Inc. was a super mini-computer company with $22 Million in sales. In 1977 the book's author, Howard Haller (who had twelve years' experience in bank leasing and equipment finance) who worked for PR1ME, created and co-found the intrapreneurial PR1ME Captive Leasing Division.

PR1ME Leasing allowed increased computer sales by providing creative alternative financing which shortened the sales cycle. PR1ME Leasing became a marketing tool to generate sales that would not otherwise have been possible.

The new finance division, PR1ME Leasing, resulted in several significant marketing and financial benefits to the parent company:

1) increased the net profit margins on computer sales

2) was quantitatively proven to materially reduce the length of the sale's cycle for the computer salesforce.

3) portfolio of equipment leases was built to over $100 million in annual volume with no cash equity contribution from the parent company, PR1ME Computer Inc. This was all accomplished totally with Non-Recourse Bank debt. Additionally, there was no contingent liability for the PR1ME leases.

4) created major tax benefits for the parent company, due to the use of the financial accounting technique of booking the revenue from the PR1ME Leases as an installment sale. This technique resulted in tens of million in deferred taxes and a significant boost in the parent company's cash flow.

5) was successfully utilizes by a statistically overwhelming

majority of the Top/Best computer sales personnel. (As defined by the highest annual sales volume that qualified for the PR1ME Computer Million Dollar Club.)

6) had a unique feature of being able to add additional equipment or to upgrade existing leasing equipment with no penalty.

PR1ME Computer, Inc. sales grew exponentially from $22 Million in sales to $480 Million in only four years. And became the #1 performing stock on the New York Stock Exchange for both sales increase and profit increase.

With the success of PR1ME Leasing, Haller recognized that there was a an additional growing need in PR1ME Computer, Inc. Dealer Network. Financing and leasing services by the PR1ME Computer, Inc. Dealer Network which would allow PR1ME's 3rd party dealers to access PR1ME's Leasing funds. So Haller submitted his second intrapreneurial idea as a formal proposal to PR1ME Computer Inc.'s Sr. Vice President of Marketing and Finance asking for permission to create the new PR1ME Dealer Finance and Leasing Division.

This creative venture was approved and launched in early 1980. Haller became the founder and National Director of PR1ME's Dealer Finance Leasing Division.

Amazon

"We've had three big ideas at Amazon that we've stuck with for 18 years, and they're the reason we're successful: Put the customer first. Invent. And be patient." ~Jeff Bezos, CEO Amazon

Amazon Inc., founded by entrepreneur and CEO Jeff Bezos, is a global giant that excels at innovation and experimentation to create profitable divisions within its corporation. Amazon uses intrapreneurship to expand their company and diversify what they offer their customers in terms of useful products and services to satisfy their customer's needs. Jeff has stated that focus should be on customer needs and that a company should work backwards from there to develop more of what they want. He believes that when the customer is satisfied, it is great for business.

Amazon has grown to include several new divisions and subsidiaries such as Kindle Direct Publishing and CreateSpace which have added self-publishing to their list of products and services that they offer their customers. Self-publishers can now transform their own manuscripts into printed books through CreateSpace and eBooks through Kindle Direct Publishing.

CreateSpace was created so customers could publish their material such as printed books, CDs, and DVDs for a lower cost than traditional publishing methods and sell their products on Amazon.com. They are an on-demand publisher which means that every time a book is ordered Amazon will print the book or make the CD/DVD and ship it to the customer. CreateSpace also allows publishers to retain full rights and control of their material. The Amazon subsidiary assists with the distribution of media through partners or retail outlets online, independent bookstores, libraries, retailers, and academic institutions.

Kindle Direct Publishing (KDP) was created by Amazon to compete in the eBook and eReader market. Kindle Direct Publishing is a portal for self-publishers to be able to sell their manuscripts as eBooks to be read on the Kindle eReader device or other computer devices that have internet conductivity.

As an inventor himself Jeff Bezos loves to experiment and test new ideas. He values and encourages these characteristics in his employees. He emphasizes that innovation within a corporation is experimentation and the willingness to invent. Entrepreneurs, no matter who they are, love to invent and build things. All great entrepreneurs have this programmed in their DNA. For innovative ideas to become profitable he stresses that companies must be willing to wait and observe this process for about five to seven years.

The Kindle eReader was new and innovative technology invented through this process. Kindle Direct Publishing was an idea that was created out of the need for customers to be able to publish and sell their own content for the eReader. The direct result of constant innovation is to see new ideas for products and services that ensures customers will always benefit by being offered the latest and the best technology available from the corporation.

Jeff Bezos believes experimenting is critical to innovating and he has implemented it at Amazon. It has always been an integral part of the culture at Amazon. He mentions that if processes were decentralized so that a lot of experimentation could occur without it having to be costly, the result would be more innovation. Jeff believes if one doubles the experiments performed within a year the ability to be innovative will double as well.

Anaconda-Ericsson Finance & Leasing Inc.

"A person should set his goals as early as he can and devote all his energy and talent to getting there. With enough effort, he may achieve it, or he may find something that is even more rewarding. But in the end, no matter what the outcome, he will know he has been alive." ~Walt Disney

Anaconda-Ericsson

Atlantic Richfield (ARCO) Anaconda Copper Subsidiary and Swedish telecommunications giant L. M. Ericsson began their relationship through a partnership in copper mining throughout the Western Hemisphere. Then, in July 1980 the two companies formed a new joint venture creating Anaconda-Ericsson, Inc. The initial focus of the Anaconda-Ericsson, Inc. was the production of ARCO's Anaconda's mining cable and L. M. Ericsson's PBX equipment and transmission systems. In subsequent years Anaconda-Ericsson would add computers, cell phone equipment, and other business-oriented products from the existing Ericsson Information Systems inventory to its list of marketed items.

Wang was the computer word processing system to beat in the early 1980s, and Anaconda-Ericsson, Inc., in an attempt to compete with Wang in the computer word processing market, acquired AXXA Corporation from Citicorp. At the time of the acquisition this was a solid business move for Anaconda-Ericsson, Inc. However, with the announcement of the IBM PC on August 12, 1981 everything changed. So in early 1982 Anaconda-Ericsson, Inc. reached out to Howard Edward Haller, a management consultant known for his solid, high tech marketing and finance experience. With a system cost of $40,000, and the ability to only handle word processing and electronic document filing, the AXXA system was both too expensive and out of date. The IBM PC employed more advanced, modern, technology at a much lower price point. Haller's recommendation was obvious – close the entire AXXA operation.

It didn't take long for Haller to successfully liquidate the AXXA operation. By mid-1982 all existing AXXA inventory had be sold to AT&T and Pacific Bell. Initially closed down, the automated computer manufacturing facility was later leased to Corona Data Systems, Inc.

Creating a "de novo" Intrapreneurship Venture.

With the successful liquidation of the AXXA division behind him, Haller presented a formal business plan to create a Western Hemisphere Captive Finance and Leasing subsidiary for Anaconda-Ericsson, Inc., ARCO, and L. M. Ericsson. His primary motivation for developing this plan was rising interest rates, including bank prime rates, and the negative impact this rise was having on Anaconda-Ericsson's cell phone broadcasting system and PBX switchboards. Haller designed and created "de novo" and intrapreneurship venture he called the "Western Hemisphere Finance and Leasing Subsidiary" whose primary focus would be to finance sales of the AEIS's products internationally. Anaconda-Ericsson Inc.'s Board of Directors and the Managing Directors approved the business proposal and appointed Haller the Managing Director (the European title for Chairman and CEO) of the new wholly owned subsidiary, Anaconda Ericsson Finance and Leasing, Inc. focused on the sales in the Western Hemisphere.

With a solid business plan behind them and Haller at the helm Anaconda-Ericsson Leasing & Finance, Inc. was able to borrow in excess of $300,000,000 on a non-recourse basis from a group of major banks with only a minimal investment by Anaconda-Ericsson Inc. In addition, the banks did not require any parent company (ARCO or L. M Ericsson) guarantees on the bank debt to fund the newly created innovative captive equipment leasing subsidiary. They also used well over $100 million of low interest debt, called "SEK debt" (Swedish Ex-IM Bank funding for export sales as the debt sources at low interest rates), to structure leverage leases and increase Anaconda-Ericsson Inc.'s sales and fund the Anaconda-Ericsson Finance and Leasing subsidiary's sales and profits.

With the assent in the market of new long-distance carriers, and their need for new long-distance network equipment, the transmission operations arm of Anaconda-Ericsson, Inc. was an immediate success. Anaconda-Ericsson, Inc.'s equipment was the right product at the right time, but what truly drove their success was the captive financing source they created. This made is much easier to implement a shorter selling cycle, increased profits, and eliminated waiting for outside financing.

With the funding in place Anaconda-Ericsson Finance and Leasing Inc. was able to finance more than $600 million of Anaconda-Ericsson's equipment in 36 months. Anaconda-Ericsson Finance and Leasing was focused on the L. M. Ericsson's MCI TELECOME equipment, PBX equipment, and Anaconda Wire & Cable equipment.

At the same time that Anaconda-Ericsson Inc. was utilizing intrapreneurship ventures to build their company, Apple Computer was also using intrapreneurship for the creation of Apple's Macintosh computer. Intrapreneurship is now a primary force to help firms grow within the United States and around the world during the early to mid-1980's.

Intel

"The future is going to be awesome because people build the future. Technology doesn't get to decide. People get to decide."
~Brian David Johnson, Intel

The Intel Corporation is an industry leader in innovation. They are no strangers to the concept of change. As experts in the field of the semiconductor, communication, and computing devices, they have kept re-inventing themselves and what they do since the late 1960s. Intel's desire to constantly improve existing products and to develop new products, have satisfied both commercial and personal computing buffs worldwide.

Intel is a multinational corporation that was founded in 1968 and is headquartered in Santa Clara, CA. It was founded by Robert Noyce and Gordon Moore innovators of the semiconductor. The name Intel was derived from Integrated Electronics and refers to its intelligence information. Based on its revenue Intel is the most prominent manufacturer of semi-conductor chips in the world. Intel creates and sells a variety of products such as network interface controllers, chipsets for motherboards, flash memory, embedded processors, graphic chips, and integrated circuits. Other products include communication and computing devices.

Intel is best known in the business world for their innovation, cutting edge manufacturing, and advanced design for computer chips. Their first product, the static Random Access Memory (SRAM) chip released in 1969, and their early design of the DRAM memory chip put them on the map. These chips made up the majority of their profit until 1981. They also produced the 1024-bit Read-Only Memory (ROM).

Intel used intrapreneurship to help catapult them into a new direction. To open up new opportunities executives at Intel were able to envision how their semiconductors could be applied within products commercially within the personal computer industry. From this necessity they were able to develop a processor that could be used in other applications as well.

The Intel 4004 Processor

In 1971, the first commercial microprocessor the Intel 4004 was created and built. Marcian "Ted" Hoff, an electrical engineer, Federico Faggin, and Masatoshi Shima of Busicom were the chief designers of the Intel 4004 chip. Ted Hoff realized that instead of utilizing a variety of custom circuits it was more efficient to use a dynamic processor that had the architecture of a single chip.

Federico Fagan, an addition to the newly established Intel MOS Department, was the first to recognize that Intel's new silicon MOS could be designed as a single chip Central Processing Unit (CPU), a random logic design methodology that is based on a silicon gate. Federico Fagan took his innovative idea and developed a universal microprocessor, a silicon chip with 2000 transistors. Masatoshi Shima designed the firmware for the calculator that was installed into the Busicom Calculator 141~PF. The combined efforts of these three individuals resulted in the super processor known as the Intel 4004.

The Intel 4004, described as a 4~bit central processing unit (CPU), was released in March 1971 as a complete CPU on one chip. It was the first commercially available microprocessor. The new silicon gate technology allowed for more transistors to be integrated within the chip. As a result of this new technology a faster processing speed could be achieved. Intel followed this chip with an 8 bit microprocessor the following year. In 1974, the 8080 which contained 40 pins, separated the data and address buses and allowed simpler and faster access to memory.

A Shift to the World of Personal Computing

Intel shifted their focus from developing SRAM and DRAM memory chips to personal computing; manufacturing and marketing their microprocessors for personal computers as their primary business. In the 1990s, the corporation created new processor designs that fueled the growth of the industry. A marketing campaign using the phrase "Intel Inside" and its Pentium Processor established Intel as a household name.

In 2012 Intel began manufacturing a new transistor known as the Tri-Gate transistor that delivers better performance and overall efficiency. This technology was used in their third generation of core processors. They have also revealed their new fourth generation core processors.

New Technology using Innovation and Intrapreneurship

Intrapreneur and futurist at Intel, Brian David Johnson, who works specifically on how people will use and interact with technology in the world of the future stresses that it is the innovation and risk taking of individuals, such as intrapreneurs within corporations like Intel, who are creating what the world of tomorrow will look and feel like.

His vision of the future includes humans living within a world that has been profoundly altered by technology. The most important innovation he sees is the size of the microchip approaching 5 nanometers or 12 atoms across by the year 2020. He also sees humans living in the midst of the great power of computation. People will be "surrounded by intelligence" and "you will be living in a world where you are essentially living in a computer."

He also envisions technology on a macro scale that includes the creation of the mega cities of the future. He sees the computers that will be built ten years from now allowing humans to build more sophisticated and larger cities. Cities will not only become greener but also become more efficient with the methods by which they manage their resources such as electricity and water. These super computers will be able to detect, monitor, and prevent waste in resources.

Corona Data Systems Inc. (Private Label IBM PC Clone Division)

"Cherish your visions and your dreams, as they are the children of your soul; the blueprints of your ultimate achievements."
~Napoleon Hill

In 1983, Haller, as a Director of Corona Data Systems, convinced Dr. Robert Harp (Corona's Chairman & CEO) and the Corona Board of Directors to allow him to build the "Private Label IBC PC Compatible Division" for Corona Data Systems Inc. This new division allowed Corona to market to major international computer mainframe manufacturers to allow Corona Data Systems Inc. to build them "Private Label IBC PC Compatible" computers, both desktop and large "portable" computers.

Howard Haller was extremely successful at closing major computer companies to buy the new Corona Data Systems Inc. "Private Label IBC PC Compatible" computers in large quantities. This massive success was in part attributed to Haller's innovative idea that Corona Data Systems Inc.'s name not appear on any part or component of the computer, nor on the operating manuals or instructions. All computers would all be transparently "Private Label" computers.

The intrapreneurial creation of Corona Data Systems Inc.'s "OEM Private Label Division" was formed specifically to market the new "Private Label" IBM PC compatible desktops and portable PC's to major international main frame computer manufacturers in Europe and the United States. These computer manufacturers [including international computer giants such as Olivetti (Italy), Phillips NV (Holland), Esselte (Sweden), Micom (Canada), and Sperry Univac (United States and Europe)] signed contacts for 10,000 to 43,000 units of the Corona Data Systems Private Label IBM Compatible PC's which brought in $180 Million in sales.

Note: *Howard Edward Haller was Co-Founder and Director of Corona Data Systems Inc.'s "OEM Private Label Division"*

LinkedIn

"If you are not embarrassed by the first version of your product, you've launched too late." ~Reid Hoffman, Founder of LinkedIn

LinkedIn has integrated intrapreneurial values in all levels of their corporate structure. They have built a culture where all employees participate in innovation. Employees and executives alike know and comprehend the importance of intrapreneurship because it is already an important facet of operations within the corporation. Executives offer support in the form of time at work and other resources to assist in the innovative efforts of key employees and some may also participate in the process of an idea through its fruition as a product or service.

LinkedIn boasts a formal program called "InCubator" where employees can create a new idea one time each quarter. Ideas are first thought of and presented at "hack days" that groups of employees attend on a monthly basis. Employees can win prizes and awards for their written software. These ideas are developed further into prototypes and are presented to an executive team. At this stage, the prototype undergoes two separate rounds of judging. The final round of judging involves both the Founder, Reid Hoffman and Jeff Wiener, the CEO. Teams whose ideas have been chosen and approved by the executive team are given three months of work time to transform their innovative ideas into a beneficial venture for the corporation.

The direct result of a successful intrapreneurship program is constant innovation. This constant flow of ideas has yielded new products and services for their customers. LinkedIn recognizes the contributions of their employees by giving them awards for the software they have written and by approving worthy projects. The corporation allows their employees to take ownership of their ideas and gives them the time and resources they will need to successfully develop a product or service that the corporation can then offer to their customers.

Lockheed "Skunk Works ®"

"Be Quick, Be Quiet, And Be On Time"
~Clarence "Kelly" L. Johnson, Lockheed "Skunk Works ®"

As early as 1943, at the height of World War II, the U.S. Army's Air Tactical Service Command (ATSC) had a dire need to create a jet fighter capable of countering the rapidly growing threat from German jet fighters. ATSC officials met with executives of Lockheed Aircraft Corporation to discuss this most important of endeavors.

It only took one month after that history U.S. Army ATSC and Lockheed meeting for a Lockheed engineer, Clarence "Kelly" L. Johnson and his team of bright young engineers to hand deliver their proposal for the new XP-80 Shooting Star Jet Fighter to the ATSC. ATSC immediately greenlit the project and Lockheed started developing the United States' first jet fighter. This historical impact of this intrapreneurial venture cannot be overstated. For it marked the birth of Kelly Johnson's corporate entrepreneurial group, the famous Lockheed "Skunk Works ®," a classic example of intrapreneurship in action.

The XP-80 Fighter; An Intrapreneurial Success

With no space available at the Lockheed facility for Johnson's "Skunk Works®" group, the Intrapreneur Kelly Johnson was forced to work apart from the corporate environment. Johnson and his hand-picked team of Lockheed Aircraft Corporation engineers and manufacturing people went to work on the XP-80 Fighter project for the U.S. Army far removed from the corporate suits, bean counters, and "by the book" Lockheed engineers. This freer and more open environment worked in "Skunk Works®" favor as they operated out of a rented circus tent.

Guided by intrapreneurship principles and "out of the box" unconventional thinking, the operation took off. This new way of thinking allowed Johnson and his "Skunk Works®" team to create and operate more effectively and efficiently than the old mode of thinking would allow.

By throwing out the Standard Operating Manual, breaking nearly all the rules, and actively challenged the corporate bureaucracy they were able to design, and build, the XP-80 in only 143 days – a full seven days before delivery to ATSC was expected. An achievement that would have impossible under the old system.

Intrapreneurship; Important Conclusions

It's been more than 60 years since Kelly Johnson came to several important conclusions which are important to every intrapreneurship venture. The official "Skunk Works®" motto underlies the entire intrapreneurship mentality "quick, quiet, and quality." Lockheed "Skunk Works®" proved that an intrapreneurship venture which was innovative and independent, could be a resounding success. By eliminating corporate "red tape" and launch a new project without a formal contract and without the formal bidding process or written agreement, they were able to do the impossible.

Intrapreneurs around the world should look to Kelly Johnson as the inspiration for the forward "out of the box" intrapreneurship spirit that was exhibited and fostered at "Skunk Works®" long before the term "intrapreneurship" was ever thought of – that would have to wait for more than thirty years.

W. L. Gore

"It is commitment, not authority, that produces results." ~William Gore, co-founder W. L. Gore & Associates

W. L. Gore (maker of Gore-Tex™- including their line of Gore-Tex rain gear) is well known for using their custom designed special materials in the manufacture of their main line of unique weather proof outdoor clothing products and other products made with their proprietary Gore-Tex material.

W. L. Gore has a program to encourage its employees to develop new ideas for the firm. The company calls its inspiring intrapreneuring program, "Dabble Time Policy." This policy allows employees to devote 10% of their time at work to their creative intrapreneurial projects.

In the middle 1990's, Dave Myers (the product creator), Chuck Hebestreit (the guitar expert), and John Spencer (the marketing genius) helped W. L. Gore launch the new brand of ELIXIR Strings which has become one of the top selling brands in the guitar string market!

Dave Myers, who worked on plastic heart implants for W. L. Gore, had an idea to coat the gear cables of his mountain bike with a thick layer of plastic to make the gears shift more smoothly. His experiments led to the creation of the "Ride-On" line of bike cables. (This unprofitable line was later discontinued.) However, while working on improving cables that controlled large animated puppets, such as the kind used at Disney World and Chuck E. Cheese's Dave needed some smaller cables and, relying on his previous experiments with coating bike cables, tried coating guitar strings with plastic. As he was coating the strings for the puppets the thought came, could these new "strings" be used for guitars?

Myers knew another Gore employee, Chuck Hebestreit, was a guitarist. He sought out his expertise and the two became a team. They experimented on the new guitar strings for over two years. Later, John Spencer, who had just finished launching W. L. Gore's "Glide" (a new line of dental floss), joined the tiny group. The trio then persuaded a few more co-workers to use their "dabble-time" to help improve the strings. After three years the team asked for the official support of W. L. Gore so they could launch their product.

Spencer and his team conducted extensive field market research of over 15,000 guitar players about their guitar strings and their guitar string wishes. The results of the extensive field marketing tests led Dave Myers and John Spencer to their "ah ha" moment. They concluded that by coating the strings for longer better sound and longer useful life that they could quickly take a major market share of the guitar string market. Though the new ELIXIR coated strings were only slightly more comfortable to play than the conventional non-coated strings, the important marketing point was that ELIXIR coated guitar strings kept their tone longer than the traditional guitar strings. The W. L. Gore ELIXER Guitar string line is an intrapreneurial success story.

Autodesk Buzzsaw.com
"Innovation is the central issue in economic prosperity"
~Michael Porter

Autodesk, a multinational software company produces
3~dimensional design software for engineering, construction,
architecture, media, entertainment, and manufacturing. Founded
before the advent of the internet it has sold millions of software
units to date. It is presently the third largest software company in
the world. In March 2008, Autodesk was one of the corporations
named to Fast Company's list of "The World's 50 Most Innovative
Companies."

Autodesk has become well-known in the corporate world for its
successful intrapreneurship strategies and for setting the standard
for encouraging and supporting an intrapreneurial culture. John
Pittman, Vice President for Autodesk, mentioned that the
environment has improved for internal entrepreneurship
(intrapreneurship.) He also states that *Autodesk Ventures* was the
starting point for many new ideas. Autodesk started the journey of
acquiring a variety of already established technologies and
establishing new divisions or expanding divisions within the
corporation. One example of this business strategy was the
acquisition of Buzzsaw.com to the AEC or Architecture,
Engineering, and Construction division of the corporation.

In June 1999, Autodesk assembled a team of employees to work
on a business plan for the acquisition of Buzzsaw.com. The plan
was "incubated" by team members for six months. Buzzsaw.com is
a website that offers the construction industry access to cloud
based software that allows teams working on projects to centralize,
exchange, and synchronize information. The software includes
model, document, and data management tools that support BIM
(Building Information Modeling) workflows. The software allows
users to access information from the Web, a computer, or a mobile
device. Buzzsaw.com includes the ability to view Revit Navisworks
models and automatically syncs files from mobile devices from any
location at any time.

Buzzsaw.com is a successful investment for its parent company. Autodesk's stock price soared shortly after Buzzsaw.com was first released on the internet. The website has earned over $90 million in capital since its release. Buzzsaw.com's success is mainly due to the transition to cloud based services. Many of the customers using Buzzsaw.com enjoy accessing and managing information on a secure cloud service over the Internet. They also find the mobile app convenient and easy to access on Apple and Android devices.

Autodesk also created a successful intrapreneurial structure within their corporation. They encouraged the development of a "catalytic" environment that boosts the morale of their employees and helps with the retention of their talented individuals for a longer span of time. Corporations, through the retention of key employees, ensure that their employees are satisfied, innovation is continuous, and customers will have new products and services to use in the future.

Yahoo!

"The world is but a canvas to the imagination."
~Henry David Thoreau

Yahoo! was able to transform disappointing earnings into profit with the advent of the sponsored search engine that was spearheaded by Scott Gatz, former Senior Director of Advanced Products and intrapreneur for Yahoo! In his blog, he stresses that he joined Yahoo! because they allowed him to be entrepreneurial within a large sized corporation. He had given serious thought to initiating his own startup or joining others just starting their own business.

He came to the self-realization that he had been an intrapreneur having had ample experience with big companies and startups during his career.

He states that the biggest impact he made in his career was taking over the Yahoo! search engine. He mentions that the corporation at that time made 50% of what was made the previous year, and the situation continued to get worse in the following months. The thinking during this time was that the company change the engine to search only what was in the directory and generate money by forcing every website in the directory to pay an annual fee. After careful deliberation, he and his team immediately worked on implementing a full web search with listings that were sponsored. He met with a Yahoo! executive and showed how he and his team could make this happen within a short time span. He also demonstrated how the sponsored search engine could generate more revenue for the company. The executive agreed to his proposal and allowed them the opportunity to carry out their business plan. They were also given a few employees to help develop the new project.

Scott Gatz emphasizes that it was interesting to witness a large company such as Yahoo! change their thinking. Affected by the dot com crash, Yahoo! moved quickly to reestablish themselves and to move forward. He states that he was happy that his intrapreneurial spirit made this venture happen and he was excited to learn new things, play with new ideas, and find the next big idea for Yahoo!

Scott Gatz is an exemplary intrapreneur who received fulfillment from his position as the Senior Director of Advanced Products at Yahoo! He has demonstrated that he is an asset to his company and that he can make a profound difference through his innovative ideas and creativity. He was also able to boost profits at Yahoo! in the long term with a new and successful business strategy in a relatively short amount of time. This sponsored project has brought in hundreds of millions and eventually billions of dollars.

Marissa Mayer, formerly a senior executive at Google, is now the President and CEO of Yahoo! She is a major advocate of intrapreneurship. Mayer is actively working to change the culture of Yahoo! and is already making innovative changes at Yahoo!

Texas Instruments

"Just as energy is the basis of life itself, and ideas the source of innovation, so is innovation the vital spark of all human change, improvement and progress" ~Ted Levitt

Texas Instruments is known for its intrapreneurship efforts within their company. The corporation leverages human capital to grow its product lines and sustain its profitability. The organization, like many companies, promotes its intrapreneurs to lead positions within their new product divisions. These talented and proven individuals have spent ample time inventing new technologies and products that have propelled Texas Instruments from a manufacturer of semiconductors to a global corporate giant. It is the third largest manufacturer of semiconductors in the world, the second biggest producer of microchips, and the largest supplier of digital signal processors and semi-conductors.

Digital Light Processing is a type of technology for projectors that uses a digital micromirror device or DMD. This novel technology was first developed in 1987 by inventor and intrapreneur Dr. Larry Hornbeck of Texas Instruments. It was applied to a variety of products such as front projectors for classroom and business use. It has also been used for rear projection of digital light in televisions and digital signs. The technology has been used in a wide variety of traditional displays as static in nature and also in interactive displays. Digital Light Projection is used in digital cinema projection.

Intrapreneurs such as Larry Hornbeck are encouraged and supported by Texas Instruments to spend time at work to create new technologies that benefit the company. Dr. Hornbeck (BA, MA and PhD in Physics) is the inventor, engineer, and intrapreneur who lead his team in the discovery of DMD technology in 1987. A Digital Micromirror Device or DMD is the heart of DLP technology. He worked on DLP technology for 20 years; he received a patent for DMD technology, and has also invented and patented various other DMD products.

He was named the Texas Instruments Fellow of 1993 and was appointed the head of the corporation's new Digital Light Production division. The U.S. government's Defense Advanced Research projects started its research in video (hi-definition). They awarded a contract of several million dollars to Texas Instruments to develop these projects. A new venture called the Digital Image Venture project was created by the corporation and Dr. Larry Hornbeck was appointed its leader in charge. Dr. Hornbeck and his team were able to develop a digital projector that was no more than five pounds and that quickly became the standard in the industry. The product successfully dominated the projector market and was able to compete within the market for HDTVs. Dr. Hornbeck's division was also able to shrink the size and the cost of a 50 lb. projector and its cost. The price of their digital projector was significantly less than the average cost of $15,000.

Texas Instruments is and continues to be a global leader in using intrapreneurship to grow their corporation through the establishment of new divisions to create new technology products. The company also leverages the talent of their corporate entrepreneurs by promoting them and appointing them to lead management positions in their newly established divisions. Texas Instruments has demonstrated that intrapreneurship is a successful business strategy in boosting and sustaining profits over a long period of time.

General Electric

"If you pick the right people and give them the opportunity to spread their wings and put compensation as a carrier behind it you almost don't have to manage them." ~Jack Welch, Former CEO of General Electric

When Jack Welch spoke to students at Nova Southeastern University's School of Business and Entrepreneurship, he said that it was his goal to make the various divisions at GE more entrepreneurial. Intrapreneurship was the model that accomplished this.

General Electric (GE) is and has been an innovative powerhouse. It is a Fortune 500 company and is the 26th largest company in the United States. It is the 14th most profitable corporation and has a long history of transforming ideas into profitable products and ventures. It was incorporated in Schenectady, New York and is presently headquartered in Fairfield, Connecticut. The corporation is divided into four important segments ~Energy, Technology Infrastructure, Consumer and Industrial, and Capital Finance.

General Electric was established by the merger of Edison General Electric Company of New York with the Thompson-Houston Electric Company of Lynn, Massachusetts. This merger occurred with the financial help of J.P. Morgan and Anthony J. Drexel. GE became a publicly traded company and was one of the original 12 companies making up the Dow Jones Industrial average.

Today GE is referred to as a multi-national conglomerate, a global mega-corporation. It has been in operation for 107 years. The corporation describes itself as being composed of primary, stand-alone businesses. Each business itself is a vast enterprise.

Re-focusing on Profitability

In 2011 GE re-evaluated the financial health of its overall business proceedings and through a series of strategic acquisitions, selling non-performing assets and reorganizations, it re-focused on the businesses and the technologies that would drive their economic growth for the next decade. By making these decisions the corporation could concentrate on the assets that had a proven track record of profitability and allow for continued growth of an already multimillion dollar business. Calculated business moves such as this help to solidify their position as a global leader in this sector of the market.

GE's businesses have varied greatly over time because of its frequent business dealings such as acquisitions, reorganizations or selling of certain assets. These assets were carefully scrutinized and categorized into profitable and unprofitable assets. For the corporation to sustain their profitability, they were willing to eliminate business ventures that had not been profitable or would not be profitable in the future. By cutting their losses sooner rather than later, they are able to redirect cash flow into expanding existing divisions, creating new ventures, or funneling more resources to innovation.

In 2002 GE was active in acquiring a number of companies as assets. GE previously sold but reacquired RCA in 1986 for the NBC television network. In 2002 GE Wind was established when Enron sold its wind turbine manufacturing assets. In 2004 it acquired 80% of Universal Pictures from Vivendi. In 2004 GE completed the creation of a company consisting of most of its mortgage and life insurance assets called Genworth Financial. In May 2007 GE purchased Smiths Aerospace for $4.8 billion. In 2010 GE purchased a gas engine manufacturer called Dresser, Opal Software, and retail credit cards from Citigroup.

Continual Innovation at GE

GE is continuously allocating resources and leads innovation efforts to increase profitability and growth in both their jet engine and health care sectors. Every year GE has funneled a little over $1 billion to jet research and development programs. The corporation has constructed a state of the art test facility in Peebles, Ohio for the final assembly and testing of their newly built commercial jet engines. Employees spend a minimum of 150 hours of rigorous testing for each of the engines. The tests simulate real world weather events such as ice storms, hail, and wind speeds of over 100 MPH. Over 1,400 jet engines are constructed at this test facility every year.

The Healthcare sector of GE is in the midst of developing an intelligent hospital robot system to sort and sterilize hospital tools. GE and the Department of Veteran's Affairs have become partners to make this system a reality. GE has used some of the same technologies that have been helping to automate manufacturing lines. This is a new application for these technologies within the context of the operating room. Their joint goal is to help make operating rooms more efficient, save millions of dollars in health care costs, minimize infections, streamline patient scheduling, and ensure better health outcomes for patients after surgery.

Many hospital staff members inspect, sterilize, and count tools manually or by hand. This strategy has proved to be time consuming and inefficient. The new GE system will be able to track tools such as clamps and scalpels with unique IDs. The tools will be sterilized and delivered at the correct time and in the correct order during surgery thereby improving efficiency during surgery.

The market for minimally invasive devices for surgery and other equipment is expected to grow by a minimum of 46% over the next five years. Hooman Hakami, President and CEO of Interventional Systems at GE Healthcare, has overseen the planning and construction of GE's new x-ray image guiding system, the Discovery IGS 730, for physicians to perform minimally invasive procedures. He states that this machine will "help revolutionize minimally invasive imaging," allowing physicians to access the body through tiny incisions. This method of surgery is quickly becoming the favored method for treating life threatening conditions that have been addressed through major surgeries.

Newell Rubbermaid

"Innovation is the creation of the new or the re--arranging of the old in a new way." ~Michael Vance.

Rubbermaid is a leading manufacturer of innovative and superior quality home, commercial, juvenile, and infant related products. The corporation includes the brands Rubbermaid, Graco, and Little Tikes. The corporation was and still is a trailblazer for innovation. It has lead and maintained a strong intrapreneurship program to allow employees, as well as the general public, to submit ideas for new products.

Rubbermaid was first founded in 1920 as the Wooster Rubber company. In 1933, James Caldwell and his wife developed and received a patent for their invention of the rubber dustpan. They subsequently developed more rubber kitchen products and named the line Rubbermaid. In 1934, the Rubbermaid Corporation and brand name was developed through a merger of the Wooster Rubber company and the Rubbermaid line of products.

In 1999 Rubbermaid was purchased by the Newell Corporation doubling the effective size of the corporation. The name was changed to Newell Rubbermaid to reflect the new merger.

Newell Rubbermaid supports and nurtures its employees by boasting an intrapreneurship program that allows employees 25% of their work time to create new and innovative products. Their intrapreneurship program will drive the development of five new lines of products to be released in 2014.

One of Newell Rubbermaid's biggest goals is to accelerate their growth into a larger, more profitable, and faster growing global company. The new Growth Game Plan focuses on consumer brands and professional brands. They describe consumer brands as goods that are marketed and directly sold to consumers while professional brands are marketed and sold to users, distributors and purchasers. The corporation is committed to using 30% of their profits to advance their innovation efforts and develop new lines of products.

Their growth plan will use intrapreneurship as a means to effectively incubate corporate growth and emerging market expansion. They consider the most efficient choices for the allocation of resources for investing in their brands. Some of their businesses such as Rubbermaid Healthcare and Endicia will receive nurturing and support to develop into growth platforms.

They have aligned their corporation's philosophy for growth around five goals:

- Make existing brands matter by innovating and producing products that are superior in both performance and design.

- Build a powerhouse for execution through the development of meaningful partnerships with their client base.

- Unleash capacity for growth that has remained untapped. Costs that are unproductive are transformed into fuel for innovating, creating, and marketing new products.

- Develop a team that can drive growth. They will attract, retain, and develop key talent.

- Extend the corporation's influence customers and expand into emerging markets for the highest potential of growth.

Rubbermaid has always been a corporation encouraging innovation. They are presently adding a new, formalized role to their corporate structure to advance and help accelerate their innovation efforts. Newell Rubbermaid has appointed Nate Young as the new Vice President of Global Innovation. This is a new position created by the corporation for energizing the company's innovative funnel. The Chief Design and R & D Officer, Chuck Jones, of the corporation states that, "Nate has already been intimately involved with Newell Rubbermaid, having led a successful series of innovation workshops for our business segments that generated hundreds of promising ideas. His familiarity with our Growth Game Plan and unique, diverse, and rich experience across the corporate, consulting, and education sectors make him the ideal candidate to lead our innovation efforts."

Both Nate Young and Chuck Jones will base their operations out of the new Design Center which is currently being built in Kalamazoo, Michigan. They will head the corporation's effort to build a network and a community of corporate and university inventors.

Sun Microsystems, JAVA

"People think of security as a noun, something you go buy. In reality, it's an abstract concept like happiness. Openness is unbelievably helpful to security."
~James Gosling, Sun Microsystems

Java was created by intrapreneurs James Gosling, Patrick Naughton, and Bill Joy. Gosling had created a programming language that was object-oriented. Gosling was a colleague at Sun Microsystems. Java had evolved from a program called Oak.

Patrick Naughton, an employee of Sun Microsystems, told the CEO of Sun, Scott McNealy, he was leaving the company. An up and coming 25~years~old Naughton was programmer who did his job very well.

McNealy saw the potential of Naughton's capabilities through his previous job performance and asked Naughton what the company was doing wrong, from his own point of view. In a 12~page email assessing what the company was doing wrong and what could be done to change it Naughton told McNealy that Sun was missing out on the fastest growing PC market for consumers. That email was a fuse that lit the dynamite for a major change. Naughton had unintentionally challenged the company to rethink their products and ideas. Scott McNealy and other corporate leaders saw the entrepreneurial abilities of Naughton and the leadership skills he exhibited on the job.

Scott McNealy encouraged Naughton to stay at Sun Microsystems. Naughton was delighted to work on his idea and see his baby created and further developed. Sun had just set out on a new adventure using intrapreneurship to move ahead of competition.

Sun organized a group that included Naughton, James Gosling, and Bill Joy. Sun recognized each member of the group due to their vision, passion, drive, and innovation. The group worked closely together and utilized their skills and talents to generate an outstanding intrapreneurship program. Both Sun and the intrapreneurs knew it was a risk. Yet Sun believed in the group and their capabilities. Sun also knew in order to remain in the competitive market they needed to introduce new products that would stand above the competitors.

Gosling had been working on a program called Oak. Oak later become known as Java. At the time, Oak was intended for Time Warner's cable boxes as part of the set-up. The deal fell through and Sun thought about abandoning the project. The group worked together on Oak and further expanded the capabilities of the original object-oriented programming language. Bill Joy recognized the potential for the object-oriented program and thought about the widespread explosion of the Web. He realized the program could be utilized across different platforms including cell phones, personal computers, PDA's and other upcoming technology.

Joy realized the only way for the program to succeed was to give the development kit and programming language away. By the end of 1996, a little more than year later, Java had attracted 6,000 developers and had obtained close to 100 licenses. Today, Java is a well-known programming language that is very widely used, all because a corporation recognized the need, had faith in the project team members, and were willing to take a risk. All the variables, components, and risks were well worth the effort and Java rapidly rose above the ranks of their competition. Java remains an optimum programming language today, all because of the teamwork of intrapreneurs and the trust of their corporation.

Saturn

"Twenty years from now you will be more disappointed by the things you didn't do than by the ones you did. So throw off the bowlines. Sail away from the safe harbor. Catch the trade winds in your sails. Explore. Dream. Discover." ~Mark Twain

The Saturn concept began in 1982 due to the increase in import competition. A partnership was formed to research and implement innovative methods to generate and market small cars manufactured in the U.S. Working together this partnership created a clear and distinct mission that was based on shared values and philosophy; target new customers while achieving world-class levels of customer enthusiasm through extremely high quality products. The slogan for this partnership became the "Different Kind of Company." This innovative new small car project was discussed and given the code name Saturn.

In February of 1999 a group that made history was appointed. This group of General Motors managers and staff employees came from 55 plants across 17 GM divisions. They immediately formed research teams to study intricate details and possible aspects of what Saturn had the potential of becoming.

The first demonstration vehicle was completed in September of 1984. General Motors announced the new addition to its vehicle line and began to widely publicize the finished product. History was made July of 1985 when a new intrapreneurial program was put into place after a labor agreement formed a partnership between General Motors and the UAW (United Auto Workers.)

The company's manufacturing and assembly site was chosen and established in Spring Hill, Tennessee. This auto plant balanced its technology and its employees and focused its vision on environmental stewardship and ergonomics. The environmental stewardship made it known as a green field site.

A Vehicle Concept Development (VDC) team was formed and in 1986 the first on-road car was built in 100 work days. From that point on, a number of successful concepts were applied and the

Saturn line expanded.

A number of developments occurred in 1987 including:

- Built-in thermoplastic panels
- The first SC coupe mule car was created by the Chassis Business Team
- The first 4~door pre-production model was completed
- The signature logo for Saturn was created and incorporated; a version of the ringed planet of Saturn that was a bright red with grey Saturn script.

Since then, milestones have been achieved. A new sporty wagon was presented at the Los Angeles auto show in 1993. By February 1993 the 300,000 Saturns had been sold. An intrapreneurial program had been implemented, risks were taken, and milestones were achieved. Highly intelligent employees with drive and motivation were recognized and valued for their knowledge, expertise, and new ideas.

General Motors took a chance. They knew something must change due to the competitive market and wanted to come up with an entirely new product through innovation and encouragement. A new era had begun and the customers loved it. It was a win-win situation for those who chose to partner with General Motors and for GM itself. This innovative Saturn division, along with several others GM division, such as Pontiac and Oldsmobile were shut down after the financial disaster at GM in the early 2000s.

Chapter 12

ULTIMATE KEY EMPLOYEE RECRUITING, DEVELOPMENT, AND RETENTION TOOL

"Don't be afraid to give up the good to go for the great."
~John D. Rockefeller

Stay Competitive In a Global Economy

The benefit of intrapreneurship is actually critical and of increasing importance today. A recent study by Monster.com and Millennial Branding found that 45% of Baby Boom workers and 41% of Gen X employees consider themselves entrepreneurial yet only about 25% of each group believes they now have the resources, support, and freedom to initiate intrapreneurial projects. Not surprising, about four in ten also said they do not expect to remain in their current position for the long haul.

One of the key factors that intrapreneurial employees consider when deciding to embark on a new career path is whether they are valued by their employer. One of the biggest psychological hurdles employees must face and deal with effectively is managing their own self esteem. If employees do not feel they are being supported or their ideas and opinions do not matter in the eyes of the corporation they will find other companies in which to place their loyalties.

"The mind is not a vessel to be filled, but a fire to be ignited."
~Plutarch

The ability to hire, advance, and retain key employees is a vital part of creating an effective and sustainable competitive advantage in today's business world. An intrapreneurship program can be a key part of these efforts and should be integrated fully into every organization to help ensure the critical cycle of recruitment, development, and retention continues.

Corporation, partnerships, organizations, and non-profits have used a variety of business tools to stay competitive in the global economy. Intrapreneurship allows employees with entrepreneurial and innovative skills to take calculated risks and pursue new and different opportunities within a large corporation. Strong, successful intrapreneurship programs can be used by corporations to break into new and emerging markets while diversifying what they offer. Through diversification of goods and services their likelihood for attracting and keeping a new client base is very high.

Successful intrapreneurship programs have been created with the intrapreneurial employees' needs in mind. These programs offer many benefits to their employees. They create a nurturing and supporting environment for them to thrive in creatively. They may also change their corporate policies to allow employees more freedom to create and operate new ventures that will broaden their horizons in the future.

"Only undertake what you can do in an excellent fashion. There are no prizes for average performance." ~Brian Tracy

Intrapreneurship is a powerful catalyst to drive a variety of key processes within the structure and framework of a company. Specific processes involving employee satisfaction, retention and development are a measure of how important employees are to a company. Employee satisfaction directly measures how effective a company is at making their employees feel valued. A company can use an intrapreneurship program to attract top talent and strengthen their team.

More talent reflects the potential for more innovation, and innovation is the key to sustained profitability. Intrapreneurship can be utilized as an effective internal tool to stimulate employee recruiting, development, and retention.

Employee Recruitment

"The key to successful leadership today is influence, not authority." ~Ken Blanchard

Having a culture in which intrapreneurship is encouraged can dramatically reshape and improve any company's image, on the inside as well as on the outside. This in turn makes it much easier to attract the kind of new talent that will push the program even further; as current employees enthusiastically tout the merits of the intrapreneurship program to other like-minded job seekers who target such organizations specifically for these opportunities.

A successful intrapreneurship program makes an organization a desirable establishment in which to work. One of the most important aspects job seekers look at besides a proposed salary and benefits such as health insurance and a 401K is whether or not a corporation has a strong intrapreneurship program. Prospective employees understand that some companies will offer whatever resources are available to allow them to create and pursue their own projects for the good of the organization.

Corporations, partnerships, organizations and non-profits on the search for talented individuals use intrapreneurship effectively as a recruiting tool. It becomes easier to attract established intrapreneurs from other companies who want to make a change. Many new recruits look for management teams that will be supportive of their ideas. Some may leave their current positions because their ideas were not valued or they want to embark on a new experience in order to grow professionally. They may seek new opportunities to transform their ideas into reality. Whatever the reason, intrapreneurship programs allow corporations to be presented to recruits in a positive light.

While intrapreneurial candidates may independently set their sights on companies and organizations that encourage this behavior it is equally important for intrapreneurial businesses to be pro-active in this regard. When filling open positions always include pertinent questions and relevant criteria in the interview process to help identify the most intrapreneurial candidates.

Employee Development

"If you want something new, you have to stop doing something old." ~Peter F. Drucker

An intrapreneurial atmosphere encourages a company's thinkers, innovators, and doers to step forward. Many times those who are most motivated will be individuals that management has already identified as high achievers. Other times, though, the best and the brightest may come as a surprise. Finding these gems hiding in plain sight, in fact, can be one of the most beneficial outcomes of initiating an intrapreneurial program.

Corporations and organizations that have effective programs focus on nurturing the intrapreneurial mindset by promoting values and behaviors characteristic of intrapreneurs throughout the entire corporate structure of the company. This mindset must first be allowed and encouraged by management. Policymakers must agree that intrapreneurship is an accepted core practice aligned towards the overall goals the corporation has set in place.

The mindset must also be modeled for all employees. Young employees and new intrapreneurs need to be crystal clear concerning what is expected of them. They need strong leaders to guide them through the learning process. They learn effectively through collaboration with leaders, on the job training, and through their own experience. By being able to tap into the knowledge and expertise of a veteran intrapreneur, young and new team members can learn through trial and error. As they gain more expertise and demonstrate that they have participated in a number of successful projects, they may be promoted, join the ranks of other company leaders, and earn more responsibility.

"Discipline is the bridge between goals and accomplishments"
~Jim Rohn

Ultimately, whoever emerges will give the organization or company an evolving pool of talent that exhibits prowess in certain skill sets sometimes in unexpected areas. An accountant might propose the perfect way to reach an elusive prospective market. A programmer may see ways to slice the production costs on a high demand but low margin product. A sales representative might propose a series of measures that will save time in accounting.

An intrapreneurship program can also identify weaknesses in otherwise star performers. By looking for ways to play to the strengths and improve on the weaknesses all of these individuals can be supported in order to further develop and cultivate their talents. An ongoing intrapreneur program offers an ideal opportunity for this, but more structured internal efforts will likely also benefit from employees input and participation. Both the company and the individual will continue to benefit.

Key Employee Retention

"All successful people men and women are big dreamers. They imagine what their future could be, ideal in every respect, and then they work every day toward their distant vision, that goal or purpose." ~Brian Tracy

Key employee retention within an organization or corporation is a result and measure of employee satisfaction. Research shows that intrapreneurial employees who feel fulfilled at their present positions in the workplace are more likely to stay longer than the three year average. The longevity of employees is an important factor for organizations and corporations on a variety of levels. It is costly to train and retrain employees.

It is more beneficial for a corporation to keep employees in whom they have already invested a lot of time and resources. These employees have a wealth of knowledge and expertise that can be tapped into at any time. They know the routine and have brought success to their companies by increasing their profit margins. It is more cost effective to give them what they need and keep them happy than to lose them.

Intrapreneurial employees who are stretched creatively and fulfilled emotionally from the opportunities available to them through intrapreneurial programs are more likely to remain with an organization rather than look for new challenges somewhere else. Increased internal visibility, recognition for successful efforts, and expanded opportunities for advancement add to the mix.

Employees want to feel that they are valued at the corporations or organizations they work for. Intrapreneurship programs empower employees to take ownership of their ideas of their projects, make important decisions, and solve ongoing problems. Giving intrapreneurs ownership over what they do helps them feel a sense of belonging and a sense of pride in what they accomplish.

While some turnover can be healthy in any environment too much can be greatly disruptive to a company's achievements and its employees' morale. It is also a huge drain on finances and time to find and train replacements. An organization doesn't have to continue losing its best workers. An intrapreneurship program offers employees the kind of challenges, rewards, and satisfaction they would otherwise need to seek elsewhere.

The best employees and key recruits have many offers and options. Having a successful intrapreneurship program is a significant and important recruiting, developing, and retention tool.

The more talent you have reflects the potential for innovation you can have, and innovation is the key to sustained profitability.

"We are God's gift to each other. Like a master composer, He brings all the instruments together, each with a different tone, each playing a different part, and He makes it turn out so beautifully." ~Jack Canfield

ABOUT THE AUTHOR

Intrapreneurship guru Howard Edward Haller, Ph.D. is a sought-after *real world authority* and keynote speaker who inspires business leaders serious about big growth to nourish the intrapreneurship flame to ignite innovation, create and retain key employees, unlock product creation, expand market share, and achieve and sustain higher profits within their organizations.

Dr. Haller goes beyond concept and theory of intrapreneurship. As a proven "hands on" intrapreneurship expert, he has taken multiple intrapreneurial ventures, as founder or co-founder, from Zero in sales to over Hundreds of Millions of dollars in sales-each in four years or less. Haller successfully built a series of profitable intrapreneurial (corporate entrepreneurial) entities within large and medium companies which collectively resulted in nearly $1 Billion of sales. Some of these include: PR1ME Computer, Anaconda-Ericsson Inc., and Corona Data Systems.

Called "The da Vinci of Finance" by those who know him, Dr. Haller is on a mission to light the spark and to nourish the flame of intrapreneurship by creating a million intrapreneurs, who are beating the drum for a way to create innovation within the confines of cubicle nation in a way it's never been done before, to make the world a better place.

Dr. Haller is an accomplished serial entrepreneur, including co-founding, building, taking public, and then selling the firm (for serious 8-figure cash) to Crédit Lyonnais Bank the technology firm RETIX.

Book Dr. Haller to speak at your event!
Turn the page to discover Dr. Haller's Intrapreneurship Topics

Visit: IntrapreneurshipSpeaker.com today!

INSPIRING KEYNOTE TOPICS!

THE TOP THREE SECRETS EXECUTIVES NEED TO KNOW TO IGNITE INNOVATION AND INCREASE PROFITS

Cutting-edge innovation gives an organization a competitive advantage, propels companies forward, and boosts their profitability quicker.

During this powerful game changing presentation you will learn:

• How to discover, advance, and inspire gifted intrapreneurs to cultivate innovation within your organization

• How to profit from the collective intelligence of your entire organization to generate fresh original ideas for unique, remarkable, and new significant products and services

• Why intrapreneurship is the secret to escalating and enduring profits

HOW TO BECOME A HIGHLY SUCCESSFUL INTRAPRENEUR

Bring intrapreneurship alive within your organization to ignite long-term profitability, enthusiasm, and be in a stellar position to retain a highly gifted staff.

During this exciting presentation you will learn:

• 12 strategies for intrapreneurial success. How intrapreneurs create escalating and enduring success for their organization

• The 9 habits of highly successful intrapreneurs and how you can discover and advance these key employees already working within your organization

• 7 Key steps to recruit, develop, and retain innovators so you can channel their creativity to your organization's goals and objectives.

Book Dr. Haller today to speak at your next event!

CPSIA information can be obtained
at www.ICGtesting.com
Printed in the USA
BVOW08s2113131217

502703BV00016BB/694/P